ANXIOUSLY CALM

Creating Your Best Spiritual Path

Brooke Sims

Coleman Digital Assets, LLC

For Jason

CONTENTS

ANXIOUSLY CALM: CREATING YOUR BEST SPIRITUAL PATH

PART I: UNDERSTANDING SPIRITUALITY

CHAPTER 1: THE CONCEPT OF SPIRITUALITY

1.1 Spirituality: An Overview

Are you looking for something more in life but aren't sure what that something is? Perhaps you're experiencing a deep yearning, a subtle tug towards something bigger than your current existence. Perhaps you've had moments of unexplained tranquilly, love, or connection that compelled you to investigate further. If any of this sounds similar, you're probably on a spiritual path, whether you recognize it or not.

So, what exactly is spirituality?

Spirituality is difficult to define since it is very personal and varies widely from person to person. Spirituality, at its foundation, is about connecting to something bigger than ourselves. This link transcends our daily concerns and desires, allowing us to access a source of great serenity and understanding. Some people discover it in nature, while others find it via meditation, prayer, or art.

Let me give you an example. Consider yourself on a beach just before sunrise. The world is still sleeping, and all you can hear is the gentle lapping of waves on the shore. You experience wonder as you gaze out at the immense expanse of the water and sky. You recognize how insignificant you are in the larger scheme of things, but you feel inextricably linked to the universe. A spiritual experience is this sense of amazement and oneness.

Spirituality is also concerned with the pursuit of truth and significance in our life. It assists us in answering major issues like "Who am I?" "What is my purpose?" and "How should I live my life?" For example, you may find yourself looking at the stars in the night sky after a long day. You may have a great feeling of amazement and interest when you think about the cosmos and your place in it. This need to comprehend our existence and the world around us is central to spirituality.

'Is spirituality the same as religion?' you may be wondering. Not always, to be sure. Religion can lead to spirituality, but they are not the same thing. Religion is only one aspect of spirituality. It is possible to be spiritual without being religious. You can be religious without being extremely spiritual, and vice versa.

Consider spirituality to be a river, with other religions as streams flowing into it. Each stream (religion) has its own distinct qualities, but they all flow into the same river (spirituality). The river represents the wider connection to the universe or a higher power, and the streams symbolize many routes to that connection.

I'd like to stress that there is no 'right' or 'wrong' way to be spiritual. Your spiritual journey is unique to you. It is a road of self-discovery, reflection, and progress. You may have times of intense joy and tranquility, as well as periods of perplexity and doubt, along the road. But keep in mind that every step you take, every question you ask, takes you closer to realizing your own spiritual essence.

In the next chapters, we will go deeper into the concept of spirituality, study various spiritual pathways, and offer advice on how to cultivate your spirituality. But for the time being, accept this idea of spirituality. Consider it. Consider how it relates to your own personal experiences and views. Most essential, pay attention to your inner voice, that subtle tug within. It could be your spirit encouraging you to go on the most rewarding adventure of your life - the spiritual journey.

Accept this trip. Believe in the process. You have arrived at your destination.

1.2 The Essence of Spirituality

After providing a general introduction to the idea of spirituality, let's proceed to a more in-depth discussion. Let's investigate the genuine nature of spirituality and get to the bottom of what makes it tick.

The concept of connection lies at the very center of spirituality. It's about having a strong sense of connection with something that's much bigger than any one of us individually. It's possible that this is a greater power, the cosmos, nature, or even the collective awareness of all living things. But it could also just be you.

Imagine, for instance, that you are strolling in a verdant and leafy forest. You can make out the rustling of the leaves, the chirping of the birds, and the soft cracking of the tree limbs as they move gently in the wind. You get the sense that you are contributing to something that is so much more significant than the day-to-day worries and your own individual existence. The forest, in all its splendor and intricacy, flourished long before you were born and will do so for a good deal of time after you are gone. Nevertheless, at this very second, you are present, you are a part of it, and you are connected. That is the essence of spirituality.

Self-awareness and maturation of the self are also significant themes in spirituality. It's a journey inside, away from the societal labels and roles that we so frequently associate with, toward a better understanding of who you truly are as an individual. It's about asking yourself profound and meaningful questions, such as "Who am I beyond my job, my relationships, and my achievements?" and "What is my purpose in life?"

Think back to a time when you felt like there was a gap between the person you are and the person you think you really are on the inside, and the person you are to the outside world. It's possible that you've established a successful career, but you're not happy with it. It's possible that everyone loves having you around, but deep down, you just want to be alone. These lapses in connection are frequently indications that your soul is prodding you in the direction of finding out more about yourself. You are being encouraged to shed the masks of the roles and expectations placed on you by society in order to uncover your true self. That is the fundamental principle behind spirituality.

Finding inner peace and nurturing love and compassion are also essential components of the core of spirituality. It's about learning to cultivate kindness toward oneself and others, even in the face of the upheavals and challenges that life brings.

Imagine that you are currently engaged in a heated debate with a close friend of yours. You stop what you're doing and take a few slow, deep breaths in the middle of the chaos. You can feel the wrath dissipating, and in its place, compassion is rising. You can comprehend and forgive their actions because you are able to see things from their point of view. This very instant, when one is at ease and compassionate, exemplifies what it is to be spiritual.

You might be wondering at this point, "In order to have a spiritual experience, do I have to go to a forest or wait for an argument?" The wonderful thing about spirituality is that it can be encountered at any time and in any place. It might happen over your cup of coffee in the morning, or while you're interacting with your kid, or even while you're doing the dishes. There is no one way or location that must be visited in order to experience spirituality. It is a state of being as well as a perspective on how the world should be viewed. It is making the decision to live a conscious life, characterized by a sense of connection, compassion, and curiosity.

I want you to understand that the journey toward spiritual enlightenment is a very individual one. It is different for each person. It's totally fine if your spiritual journey takes a different form than mine or anyone else's; we all walk our own unique paths. What is important is that you identify with it and that it has meaning for you. It enables you to comprehend and respect your most fundamental self. It establishes a link between you and the expansive and breathtaking cosmos that we are all a part of.

1.3 The Difference Between Spirituality and Religion

"What's the difference between spirituality and religion?" is a question people often ask. It can be hard to tell the difference between the two, but they are different ideas that can stand on their own or be linked in different ways. So, let's go on a trip to resolve these ideas and get a better grasp on them.

Imagine that you are standing in front of a beautiful, old church. The tall steeple, the elaborate carvings, and the beautiful stained-glass windows are all things that make you take notice. As soon as you step inside, you hear a quiet that tells stories of ages of faith and service. This is what faith is. It's about the past, the society, the rituals, and the rules. It's a shared set of beliefs and worship that has been passed down from generation to generation.

Now, imagine you're on top of a cliff at dawn. The soft, pink light of dawn is still shining all over the world. You feel a deep sense of peace and wonder as you breathe in the cool morning air and watch the sun slowly rise above the horizon. Spirituality is your link with nature, the universe, the divine, or whatever you think of as the bigger world outside of yourself. It's a personal, individual thing. It's a journey of self-discovery and relationship that goes beyond the physical and into the metaphysical.

Now that we've looked at these pictures, let's go into more detail.

Religion is often about belonging to a group. We all go through it together. People who believe the same things get together to worship and enjoy. Religion gives people a way to make sense of the world, live their lives, and link with the divine. Religions, for example, have holy days, traditions, and rules about how to act. These things make it possible to live your faith.

Think about going to a church service. You are surrounded by people who believe the same things you do. You pray, sing hymns, and enjoy religious holidays together. Having a feeling of belonging to a group can be very powerful. It gives a sense of connection and a network of people who can help. A big part of faith practice is getting together with other people.

On the other hand, faith is very personal. It's about your unique events and perceptions. It's about how you, as an individual, connect with the world or God. Spirituality is not limited by rules or practices. It's a free-flowing trip where you can choose your own way.

Think about a time when you felt a deep sense of peace, wonder, or connection. Maybe it happened while you were watching a sunset, looking up at the night sky, or relaxing. Spirituality can be seen in these deeply personal events. There are times when you went beyond the everyday and felt the divine. Spirituality is a journey that is different for each person.

Religion is usually based on a belief in a greater power or a divine being, which is then worshiped. This belief usually comes with a set of teachings or doctrines about how the world works, what happens after death, what is right and wrong, and so on.

Imagine a sacred book like the Bible, the Quran, or the Bhagavad Gita. These texts have teachings, stories, and instructions that help people understand and follow their views. A key part of faith is this organized set of beliefs.

On the other hand, you don't have to believe in a specific god or follow a certain ideology to be spiritual. It's more about growing as a person, learning more about yourself, and finding your place in the world.

Picture that you are doing mindfulness meditation. As you pay attention to your breath, you become very aware of the present. You understand that everything is connected, and that life is short-lived. Spirituality can be seen in this inner insight and deep understanding.

In a nutshell, religion offers a structured, communal way to connect with the divine, while spirituality is a personal, subjective journey of self-discovery and global connection.

I do want to stress, though, that faith and religion don't contradict each other. You can believe in God and be spiritual. You can follow religious rules and rituals and go on a spiritual trip of your own. In the same way, you can be spiritual but not religious. Even if you don't follow a particular church, you may still have a strong sense of spirituality.

In the big picture of life, there are a lot of different threads that show different ways to understand God and our place in the world. Some threads follow the set patterns of religion, while others make their own unique spiritual path. Each line, or thread, is valid. Each adds to the beautiful variety of what people know and what they have done.

CHAPTER 2: SPIRITUALITY AND HUMAN CONSCIOUSNESS

2.1 The Spiritual Mindset

Have you ever noticed how some people seem to shine from the inside? Even in the middle of chaos and problems, they seem to move through life with a deep sense of peace and purpose. I like to say that these people have what I call a "spiritual mindset." It's a way of thinking that changes how they see life, gives their everyday events more meaning, and helps them become their best selves. So, what is a spiritual attitude, and how do we develop one? Let's dive in.

Let's start by defining what an attitude is. A mindset is the way we think, feel, and see ourselves, other people, and the world around us. It's like the way we see and understand life through a lens. The colors of connection, kindness, gratitude, and surrender are what tint the lens of a spiritual mind. It's a way to look at and live life that goes beyond the physical and touches the divine.

Think about a beautiful sunrise you've seen. You didn't just notice the beauty and move on; you were deeply moved by it. You felt at peace, connected to the world, and thankful for the new day. This moment of spiritual understanding shows how a spiritual person thinks.

So, how do we grow a spiritual outlook? It starts with becoming aware of how we are all linked. We're all connected in a big, complicated web of life, and each thread is just as important as the others. We're all connected in many ways, whether to other people, to nature, or to the world as a whole.

Imagine you're on a train that's very busy. It's easy to see the people around you on the plane as strangers who have nothing to do with your life. But if you have a spiritual attitude, you can see that we are all the same. You know that they have hopes, dreams, fears, and problems just like you do. Recognizing that we all share the same human experience is a step toward a spiritual way of thinking.

A spiritual way of thinking also means learning to be compassionate and kind, both to us and to others. It's about realizing that everyone, including we, is doing the best they can with what they know and how their lives are going.

Think back to a time when someone treated you badly. When you have a spiritual outlook, you are more likely to react with understanding instead of anger. Maybe they're having a hard time on the inside, and their rudeness is a sign of that, not a reflection on you. When you choose to be kind instead of angry, you have a spiritual attitude.

Another important part of a spiritual way of thinking is being thankful. It's about being grateful for all the good things in our lives, no matter how small they may seem.

Think back to the last time you ate something tasty. Did you enjoy every bite, thank the food for keeping you alive, and think about the chain of events that led to your meal? A spiritual attitude includes being aware of and grateful for these things.

Lastly, a spiritual mindset means giving up and trusting that the world or a higher power has a bigger plan. It's about letting go of the need to oversee everything in our lives and learning to go with the flow of things.

Think about a time when your plans didn't work out. You didn't fight or get angry. Instead, you believed that there was a reason, even though you couldn't see it at the time. This trust and giving up is part of having a spiritual mind.

Developing a spiritual way of thinking is a process, not a goal. It's a process of learning and getting better all the time. Some days it might just feel right. On some days, it might be hard. But remember that each step and moment of awareness gets you closer to a deeper, more meaningful connection with yourself and the universe.

2.2 Consciousness and Spirituality

Now that we've looked at the spiritual attitude, let's look at awareness and its relationship to spirituality. After all, extending our consciousness is typically the first step on the way to spiritual growth.

So, exactly what is consciousness? It goes beyond simply being awake and aware of our environment. Our thoughts, feelings, perceptions, and self-awareness are all part of our consciousness. Our life experience is defined by our personal narrative.

Consider yourself to be a wide, deep ocean. The surface of the water represents your conscious mind - your current ideas, feelings, and perceptions. However, beyond the surface is another world, the subconscious and unconscious mind, which is packed with memories, experiences, and deep-seated beliefs that influence you in ways you may not be aware of. In essence, consciousness is the entire ocean, from the surface to the deepest depths.

So, how does spirituality fit into this overall picture of consciousness? Spirituality entails going beyond the surface level of everyday encounters and diving into the deeper depths of our existence. It's about going beyond the tangible and connecting with the metaphysical, the divine.

Consider a time when you were completely immersed in a magnificent piece of music. The world around you begins to vanish, and you are transported to a realm beyond your immediate physical reality. You feel a strong connection to the music, to yourself, and possibly to the universe. This transcendental experience provides a glimpse of spiritual awareness.

How can we cultivate this spiritual awareness? How do we enter the deeper reaches of our being?

The first step is to practice mindfulness. Being totally present and engaged in the present moment, monitoring our thoughts and feelings without judgment, is what mindfulness entails. It's about transitioning from autopilot to mindful living.

Consider yourself to be eating a piece of chocolate. Instead of blindly devouring it, you pause to savor it. With each bite, you notice the rich color, pleasant perfume, silky texture, and blast of flavor. This present-moment mindfulness is the first step toward expanding your consciousness.

Meditation is another effective strategy for developing spiritual consciousness. It entails quieting our minds and tuning in to our inner selves. It's all about making a sacred space for self-discovery and communion with the divine.

Consider yourself sitting in a peaceful place, eyes closed, focused on your breath. As thoughts arise, you notice them without attachment and let them drift away, like clouds in the sky. The core of spiritual consciousness is this state of inner quiet and awareness.

Compassion and empathy are also aspects of spiritual consciousness. It entails acknowledging our common humanity and reacting to the experiences of others with kindness and understanding.

Consider a time when you helped a buddy in need. You listened with empathy, put yourself in their situation, and answered compassionately. This act of comprehension and empathy reflects spiritual consciousness.

Finally, spiritual consciousness entails accepting the interconnection of everything. It's about accepting that we're all intertwined in a vast, intricate fabric of existence.

Take a look at the food on your plate. It's not simply a meal; it's the culmination of a series of events, beginning with the sun's rays nurturing the crops and ending with the farmers harvesting them and chefs cooking them. Spiritual knowledge includes recognizing and appreciating this connectivity.

It takes a lifetime to develop spiritual consciousness. It is a constant process of expanding our awareness, opening our hearts, and connecting with the divine. I encourage you to investigate your consciousness as we continue to examine spirituality in the following chapters. Be aware, mindful, and caring. Dive into the deeper parts of yourself. The road is difficult, but it is also immensely gratifying, leading to a deeper, richer understanding of life.

2.3 The Interconnection of Spirituality and The Universe

The concept of interconnectivity is at the heart of spirituality. It's the recognition that we're not isolated beings navigating our lives in solitude, but integral parts of a vast, intricate universe. This realization has profound implications for our spiritual journey, and in this chapter, we'll explore this awe-inspiring interconnection between spirituality and the universe.

Take a moment to look up at the night sky. Countless stars and galaxies, each with its planets, perhaps with life forms we can't even imagine. It's an overwhelming thought, isn't it? But here's the most incredible part: The same elements that make up these distant stars and galaxies also make up you. As astronomer Carl Sagan once said, "We are made of star stuff." In the most literal sense, we are intimately connected to the universe.

But the connection runs deeper than physical elements. Spiritually, we're tied to the universe through shared energy and consciousness. Ancient Eastern philosophies and modern quantum physics alike speak of a universal life force, a dynamic, vibrating energy that permeates all existence. Call it Chi, Prana, or the Quantum Field - this energy binds us to the universe.

To illustrate this, consider a time you walked into a room and instantly felt a 'vibe'. That's you sensing the energy. Or think about how you feel an inexplicable connection with certain people, places, or experiences. That's the shared energy resonating within you.

Our consciousness, too, interweaves us with the universe. When we expand our consciousness, we tap into the universal consciousness - the collective consciousness of all living beings and the universe itself. It's akin to realizing that our individual waves are part of a vast, boundless ocean.

Think of a time when you've experienced a synchronicity - an event that seems like a 'coincidence' but feels deeply meaningful. Like thinking of a friend, you haven't spoken to in a long time and then receiving a call from them the same day. These synchronicities are instances of our individual consciousness resonating with the universal consciousness.

Now, how does this interconnection influence our spiritual journey?

First, it fosters a sense of oneness and compassion. When we realize that we're part of the universe, and so is everyone else, we begin to feel a sense of shared existence. It becomes natural to respond to others' joys and sorrows as our own, nurturing a deep-seated compassion.

Imagine you see a stranger helping another stranger on the street. That sense of warmth and joy you feel reflects your recognition of shared oneness. Your heart recognizes the universal connection even if your mind doesn't articulate it.

Second, this interconnection inspires awe and gratitude, uplifting our spirits. Reflecting on our cosmic connection can fill us with a profound sense of awe at the universe's grandeur and gratitude for being a part of it.

Think about a time when you watched a beautiful sunset or gazed at the star-studded sky. That sense of peace, wonder, and gratitude you felt is a spiritual response to our interconnection with the universe.

Finally, embracing our universal connection can guide our life purpose. Recognizing that we're part of a larger whole can inspire us to contribute positively to the world, aligning our actions with the greater good.

Imagine realizing that a single small act of kindness, like planting a tree, can ripple outwards, affecting the environment, the animals, and people, now and in the future. This recognition can inspire us to integrate such actions into our life purpose.

Embracing our interconnection with the universe is a transformative spiritual experience. It expands our consciousness, nurtures compassion, fills us with gratitude, and guides our purpose. As we delve deeper into spirituality in the upcoming chapters, I encourage you to reflect on your connection with the universe. Feel the shared energy. Tap into the universal consciousness. Marvel at the cosmic interplay. You are an essential part of the universe, and the universe is an integral part of you. This connection is not just spiritual but also a profound truth of existence. Cherish it. Celebrate it. And most importantly, let it guide your spiritual journey.

PART II: EMBRACING SPIRITUALITY

CHAPTER 3: DISCOVERING YOUR SPIRITUAL PATH

3.1 Reflecting on Personal Beliefs

The fact that there is no single path that must be followed in order to be spiritually fulfilled is one of the many wonderful things about spirituality. It is singular and distinct, just like each one of us. Therefore, prior to embarking on our spiritual path, it is necessary to spend some time contemplating our individual convictions and values. These beliefs form the basis of how we comprehend not only ourselves but also the world and our place in it.

What exactly are some beliefs? In their most basic form, beliefs can be broken down into three categories: assumptions, perceptions, and values. They serve as the basis upon which we build our lives, exerting an influence on our thoughts, deeds, and the connections we maintain. Some of our beliefs might help us grow, while others can hold us back. However, each of our beliefs has a purpose in directing the course of our spiritual journey.

Take time to reflect about the things that you believe. In what ways do you believe life to be true? In reference to the universe? Concerning the divine? It's possible that these beliefs are articulate and well-defined in your head. Or, they could be implicit, meaning that they influence your life in a way that you are not consciously aware of.

It's possible, for instance, that you have faith in people's innate capacity for good. It is possible that this notion influences the way you connect with other people, causing you to approach them in a way that is trusting and open. Or it's possible that you have a strong faith in a higher force that not only directs your life but also provides you with solace when things go rough.

Now, how exactly do you go about unearthing these beliefs? One of the most effective methods is to engage in some self-reflection. Every day, set aside some time for reflection on how your ideas, feelings, and actions have shaped your day. Keep a journal regarding them. Over the course of time, patterns will become apparent, illuminating the beliefs that lie beneath them.

Imagine that you have identified a pattern in which you are reluctant to engage in novel events. If you dig a little deeper, you can discover that you have the belief that you are incapable or that new experiences are scary. Your spiritual journey toward growth and transformation begins with the initial step of acknowledging this concept.

It is essential to approach this investigation of beliefs with compassion and without passing judgment on the results. Remember, there's no 'correct' or 'wrong' belief. Every one of our convictions serves a function, even if it's just to point us in the direction of a more in-depth comprehension of who we are.

Personal introspection paves the way for progress along the spiritual path we have chosen. This is an invitation to gain a deeper understanding of who we are, to challenge the beliefs we have held to be true, and to be more receptive to alternative points of view. As you embark on your spiritual journey, I ask you to explore your beliefs. Approach them with an attitude of openness and interest. Treasure the wisdom that they can impart. Also, keep in mind that your spiritual journey will be entirely unique to you, as it will be shaped by the beliefs that you hold most dear. Accept it and allow it to steer you in the direction of maturation, enlightenment, and a more profound connection with the cosmos.

3.2 Exploring Different Spiritual Paths

We are now in a better position to investigate the diverse spiritual avenues open to us because we have a greater comprehension of the ideas that guide us. On our individual spiritual journeys, we can choose to travel any number of distinct routes, just as each of us is a one-of-a-kind being.

Imagine the vastness and splendor of a forest when you think about spirituality. The several paths that wind through the woods each reflect a different kind of spiritual journey. There is a way that is paved with the teachings of Buddha, another path that is paved with the wisdom of Lao Tzu, another path that is paved with the chanting of Hindu mantras, and another path that is paved with the love that Christ has for his followers. Some roads lead to the mysticism of Kabbalah, while others end in the sacred dance of Sufism. Both religions have their roots in the ancient Near East. There are other roads illuminated by the knowledge of long-standing cultures, the wondrous attractions of the natural world, and the astounding achievements of modern science. And would you believe it? You are at liberty to investigate any number of possible courses!

There is no correct or incorrect path, rather you should follow the one that feels natural to you. Your way could be defined by one of the world's main religions, an amalgamation of various tenets, a personal code of ethics, or a profound respect for the natural world. The most important thing is that it is congruent with your beliefs, that it enhances your life, and that it draws you closer to the divine, in whatever form you understand that term to be.

Take for example a person who was brought up in a Christian environment but later discovered that they were drawn to the Buddhist teachings of mindfulness. They do not have to give up their Christian roots; rather, they may create a spiritual practice that is unique to them by including mindfulness. This will allow them to follow a path that is genuine to them.

When one person is surrounded by natural beauty—such as feeling the breeze on their skin, hearing the rustle of leaves, or staring at a gorgeous mountain—another person may have a profoundly meaningful spiritual connection. It's possible that spending time in nature, being a good steward of the environment, and paying respect to the natural rhythms of the world are all part of their spiritual journey.

Others may discover their spirituality through acts of service, experiencing a strong connection with the divine as a result of the good they provide for other people. Their route to enlightenment could include activities such as volunteering, being politically active, or performing acts of compassion at random.

Keep in mind that your selection of a spiritual path is not a static decision but rather an ongoing journey. It's possible that it will shift as you gain more knowledge and experience. It's possible that you'll go on one route, only to later discover another that is more strongly connected with you. Alternatively, you may create a one-of-a-kind tapestry that symbolizes your developing spirituality by weaving together aspects of other spiritual paths.

Imagine someone who has been doing yoga for years in order to improve their physical health, but who has only recently started to explore the more spiritual aspects of the practice. Their spiritual path develops with time, allowing them to incorporate new aspects that bring them increased contentment and satisfaction.

During our spiritual journey, it is both fascinating and fulfilling to investigate the various spiritual pathways that are available to us. It not only helps us establish a route that truly resonates with us, but it also broadens our perspectives and enhances our awareness of the world. I want to urge you to keep an open mind and heart as you continue your spiritual path and discover new things along the way. Keep in mind that you are not merely picking a road; you are building your own path. You are the only one who has it, it can be edited, and it can be as fluid as you want it to be. This is your adventure, your path, and your journey through life on a spiritual level. Accept it, have fun with it, and allow it to guide you to the tremendous delight that comes from having a close connection with the divine.

3.3 Personalizing Your Spiritual Journey

If there's one thing to remember about faith, it's that your spiritual journey is yours and yours alone. It's as unique as you are. It's not about following a set of rules or ideas. Instead, it's about finding what speaks to your soul and helps you connect with the divine. Putting your own spin on your spiritual journey is a freeing process that can help you learn a lot about yourself and grow spiritually.

As we've talked about in earlier parts, start by thinking about what you believe and what you value. What facts are important to you? What ideals guide your life? These thoughts are like a compass that can help you figure out where your spiritual road might lead.

Next, think about what you like and what you tend to do. Do you like being alone and quiet, or do you find mental nourishment in being with other people? Do you feel a strong link to nature, or do you prefer the energy of city life? Do music and art move you, or does reading and writing make you feel alive?

A person who likes to be alone might make their spiritual journey more personal by meditating, walking in nature, or going on solo vacations. A church, temple, or spiritual group could be a spiritual home for someone who does better in a group. A person who loves nature might find spirituality in gardening, hiking, or looking at the stars. A person who lives in the city might find spirituality in the pace and energy of city life. A painter or musician might show their faith through their art, and a writer might write about spiritual ideas in their work.

Think about your daily life and habits as well. You can turn the things you do every day into sacred routines by adding spirituality to them. When you cook with love and thanks, it can become a form of meditation. When you work out, you honor your body's strength and energy, which can be a spiritual act. Even doing chores like cleaning can be spiritual because it helps you make a peaceful place.

Remember that there is no 'right' or 'wrong' way to make your spiritual journey your own. It all comes down to what speaks to you. Your journey might not look like anyone else's, and that's how it should be. Your spiritual path is an indication of who you really are at your deepest level.

As you move forward on your spiritual path, don't forget to be kind to yourself. Creating your own path takes a lot of trial and error, learning, and growth. You might try things that don't work for you, and that's fine. All of this is part of the trip. Every step, every new experience, and every "mistake" gets you closer to your true spiritual path.

So, I want to ask you to make your spiritual journey your own. Explore different roads, try out different ways of doing things, and think about what you've learned. Listen to your mind, your heart, and your intuition. They will help you find the ideas, practices, and paths that match your unique spiritual essence. This is where you're going. Personalize it. Treasure it. Celebrate it. And most importantly, enjoy the great adventure of finding your own spirituality and sharing it.

CHAPTER 4: THE PRACTICE OF MEDITATION

4.1 The Role of Meditation in Spiritual Growth

Meditation. It's a word we hear often in the realm of spirituality, self-help, and wellness. But what is meditation really, and how does it fuel our spiritual growth?

Meditation, at its core, is a practice of presence. It's about grounding ourselves in the here and now, setting aside the chatter of our minds, and connecting deeply with our inner selves and the universe.

How does this simple practice contribute to our spiritual growth? The power of meditation lies in its ability to shift our perspective, open our hearts, and transform our lives from the inside out.

Firstly, meditation offers us a profound sense of peace and

clarity. By quieting our mind, we step away from our day-to-day concerns, anxieties, and distractions. This mental stillness allows us to see our lives with newfound clarity. It's like wiping clean a dirty window and discovering a breathtaking view we couldn't see before. Suddenly, we can perceive our life situations, relationships, and self in a new light, guiding us to make choices more in alignment with our spiritual growth.

Secondly, meditation connects us with our true essence. In the silence of meditation, we peel back the layers of our identity - our roles, our achievements, our failures, our self-images. What remains is our true self - pure, infinite, divine. This realization is a powerful catalyst for spiritual growth. When we recognize our divine essence, we naturally begin to align our thoughts, words, and actions with this truth. We choose love over fear, compassion over judgment, and authenticity over pretense.

Thirdly, meditation strengthens our connection with the universe. In the quietude of meditation, the boundaries of our individual selves begin to blur. We sense our interconnectedness with all beings, all things, all of existence. This sense of unity is a cornerstone of spirituality. It moves us to honor all life, act with kindness and respect, and serve the collective good, enriching our spiritual journey.

Moreover, the effects of meditation extend beyond our spiritual lives. Science has shown that regular meditation can reduce stress, improve focus and creativity, enhance our emotional wellbeing, and even boost our physical health. In essence, meditation nurtures our whole being - body, mind, and soul.

Imagine the calmness of a lake at dawn, its surface smooth and serene. Now, think of a stone plunging into the lake, creating ripples that spread outwards, reaching every shore. That's the impact of meditation on our lives. It starts as a personal practice, a moment of silence and presence. But its effects ripple outwards, influencing every aspect of our lives and propelling us on our spiritual journey.

Meditation is more than a practice. It's a pathway to spiritual growth, a key to inner peace, and a tool for transformation. No matter where you are on your spiritual journey, meditation can be a powerful ally. It's a haven of tranquility in a busy world, a touchstone of clarity in times of confusion, and a bridge to our innermost self and the universe. As you continue your spiritual journey, I invite you to explore the practice of meditation. Allow it to guide you, inspire you, and propel you towards deeper spiritual growth.

4.2 Techniques for Effective Meditation

Meditation is an intensely intimate experience. It's like a lovely, peaceful garden with numerous trails winding through it. Each path symbolizes a different meditation technique, and your duty is to discover which one connects with your soul and feeds your spiritual journey.

Let's look at some of the most prevalent and efficient meditation techniques to help you explore this meditation garden. Remember, there is no such thing as a 'proper' or 'bad' technique. It's all about figuring out what feels natural, comfortable, and useful to you.

Meditation for Mindfulness

The practice of cultivating a concentrated awareness of the present moment is known as mindfulness meditation. It is about recognizing your ideas, feelings, and sensations without passing judgment.

Let's do a little mindfulness exercise. Close your eyes and sit comfortably. Allow your body to relax by taking a few deep breaths. Now concentrate on your breathing. Take note of how the air flows in and out of your nostrils. With each breath, feel your chest rise and fall. When your thoughts wander (and they will), gently bring them back to your breath. You're not attempting to stop your thoughts; instead, you're watching them with love and interest before returning your attention to your breath.

Meditation on Loving-Kindness

This practice, also known as Metta meditation, focuses on establishing a loving and gentle attitude toward oneself and others.

To begin, select a comfortable place and close your eyes. To center yourself, take a few deep breaths. Then, silently repeat loving and gentle things to yourself. "Please keep me safe," for example. "May I be well." "May I be content." "May I live in peace." Fill your heart with the warmth of these words. Once you've directed these sentences towards yourself, you can apply them to others: loved ones, acquaintances, strangers, and even those with whom you've had disagreements.

Meditation Using Mantras

Mantra meditation entails silently repeating a word or phrase to assist in focusing your thoughts and deepening your meditation.

To begin, locate a peaceful and comfortable location to sit. Take a few deep breaths and close your eyes. Choose a mantra that speaks to you. It might be a word such as "peace," "love," or "joy," or it could be a statement such as "I am calm" or "I am enough." Repeat your chant silently in your head. If your focus wanders, softly bring it back to your chant.

Remember that constancy is the key to effective meditation. Pick a technique that speaks to you and stick with it. Even a few minutes a day can have a significant impact on your spiritual development, mental clarity, and overall well-being.

Remember to be gentle with yourself while you experiment with these strategies. Meditation is a journey rather than a destination. It's all about adventure, learning, and growing. Every moment of presence, every mindful breath, every loving thought is a step forward in your spiritual journey. Accept the practice, accept the journey, and allow meditation to illuminate your spiritual path.

4.3 Meditation for Daily Life

This practice will serve as your haven, a place for you to investigate the topography of your inner world, to establish a profound connection with your essential self, and to saturate your heart with loving-kindness.

Find a place that is calm, comfortable, and undisturbed where you can sit down and start writing. You are free to sit however you feel most comfortable, be that in a chair or on a cushion on the floor. As you get yourself comfortable, allow your hands to fall lightly into your lap, close your eyes, and turn your attention inward.

Take a few calming breaths, focusing on expanding your chest and belly as you inhale with your nose and exhale through your mouth. Relax and let go of any stress that may be present in your body with each breath. Feel the connection that your body has with the earth underneath you, which will help you feel more rooted in the here and now.

Now, bring your focus softly onto the way you are breathing. Take note of its natural rhythm, the feeling of air entering and exiting your nostrils, and the gradual rising and falling of your chest or abdomen as you breathe in and out. Don't try to manipulate or control your breath; instead, focus on being a compassionate spectator of this process that keeps you alive.

It is natural for thoughts to come to mind as you become more settled into this conscious awareness. Instead of getting caught up in them and allowing them to consume you, simply acknowledge them without passing judgment on them and allow them to pass like clouds in the sky. At any time that you become aware that your mind is wandering, bring your focus back to your breath, which serves as your anchor in the here and now.

Imagine that this light is filled with love and warmth and that it is centered in the center of your chest. Imagine that this light is growing and spreading out, permeating every part of your body with loving-kindness as you take another breath. Feel this love for yourself, and acknowledge that you are worthy of this intense, all-encompassing affection.

Gradually, open to the idea that this loving light can spread beyond the confines of your physical body. Imagine it surrounding your loved ones and infusing them with the same kind heartedness and warmth as it does you. Extend this light even further, allowing it to touch the people you know, the people you don't know, and even the ones you've had disagreements within the past.

Now, picture this warm, illuminating light encompassing the whole world. Sense how all beings are intertwined with one another and how they are all a part of the same cosmic dance of love and goodwill. Spend a brief amount of time soaking in this feeling of oneness and compassion and allow it to seep into the very fibers of your being.

Take a minute to reflect on the journey you've been on as we get ready to end this meditation. I want to thank you for joining me on this path. Experience the calm that comes from practicing mindfulness, the happiness that comes from connecting with others, and the warmth that comes from being benevolent.

Begin to gradually extend the length of your breath while you bring back some soft movement into your body. Move your fingers and toes in a circular motion, and when you feel ready, start blinking your eyelids slowly open. As you move forward with the rest of your day, keep this sense of peace, connection, and love with you.

Keep in mind that this sanctuary of attention, connection, and generosity is always accessible to you; it is located within your very own heart. We are grateful that you have chosen to participate in this meditation. Be kind and patient with yourself and let the brightness of your light show.

CHAPTER 5: OTHER SPIRITUAL PRACTICES

5.1 The Importance of Mindfulness

Spirituality is like a multi-faceted gem, with each facet reflecting a distinct practice. We uncover new channels to our inner selves and the world when we turn the diamond, investigating each of these techniques. In this chapter, we'll look at mindfulness, a characteristic that shines brightly with profound simplicity and depth.

The discipline of giving complete attention to the present moment without judgment is known as mindfulness. It's about being totally present in each moment, welcoming it with openness, curiosity, and love.

What is the significance of mindfulness in our spiritual journey? Assume you're lost in thought while wandering through a wilderness. You're so preoccupied with your thoughts that you miss the sunshine filtering through the leaves, the rustle of the breeze, and the earth's aroma. You may arrive at your destination, but you have missed the voyage.

Mindfulness encourages us to be present in the now. It enables us to live life more totally, deeply, and genuinely. It assists us in recognizing the beauty, joy, and love that pervades each moment. This conscious presence enhances our spiritual journey by deepening our connection to our inner selves and the cosmos.

Take the act of eating as an example. We frequently eat while watching television, scrolling through our phones, or lost in thought. But what if we ate with intention? What if we savored each bite, focusing on the flavors, textures, and colors of our food? What if we thanked it for the sustenance it provides? This simple act transforms a mundane activity into an experience of joy, connection, and thankfulness. That is the strength of mindfulness.

Consider our interpersonal relationships. Our talks are frequently hampered by distractions or busy minds. We're physically present, but our minds are elsewhere. But what if we approached it mindfully? What if we genuinely listened, not just to answer, but to comprehend and connect? Our relationships would undergo a transformation defined by increased understanding, empathy, and love.

Mindfulness promotes inner peace and resilience as well. We may respond to life's issues with calm and clarity when we are present, rather than reacting out of habit or impulse. With an anchored heart, a clear intellect, and a steady spirit, we can traverse life's storms.

Finally, awareness provides access to our inner selves. We peel back the layers of thinking, emotion, and identity as we quiet our minds and pay attention to the present moment. We encounter our essence, that core of serenity, pleasure, and love within us. We comprehend that we are the cosmos expressing itself in human form, not just a part of it.

So, how can we practice mindfulness? The beauty of mindfulness is that it may be practiced at any time and in any place. You can choose to be present, pay attention, and completely engage whether you're eating, walking, working, or talking. Begin with little mindful moments - a mindful breath, a mindful step, a thoughtful bite - and work your way up to a mindful existence.

Remember that mindfulness is not about maintaining a permanent state of focus or calm. It's about returning to the present moment with kindness and patience over and over. It's about appreciating the trip rather than the destination.

5.2 Prayer and Chanting

Prayer and chanting have a specific position in the domain of spiritual practices. These ancient techniques, which have their roots in many spiritual traditions around the world, provide a powerful channel for connecting with your higher self, the divine, or whichever higher power resonates with you.

Let us begin with prayer. Consider prayer to be a personal discussion with the cosmos in which you communicate your deepest thoughts, emotions, desires, and aspirations. It's a place where you can bare your soul, express gratitude, seek advice, find comfort, and assert your faith.

Prayer is not restricted to any one religious belief or practice. It can be done by anybody, anyplace, and in any way that seems right to you. It could be a structured prayer with particular words and phrases, an impromptu encounter with the divine, or a silent confession of your deepest longings.

Sincerity is the most important aspect of prayer. When you pour your heart into your prayers, they transform into a powerful force, a link between you and the divine. You join the cosmos as a co-creator, connecting your intentions, actions, and energies with the flow of life.

Let's investigate chanting now. The rhythmic reciting or singing of words or sounds is known as chanting. Chanting, like prayer, is utilized in many spiritual traditions to express devotion, focus, and connect with the divine.

Religious hymns, mantras, affirmations, or sacred words can all be chanted. In the Buddhist faith, for example, practitioners frequently chant the mantra "Om Mani Padme Hum," which is thought to elicit the blessings of the Bodhisattva of Compassion. The sound "Om" is sung as a depiction of the divine in its wholeness in Hindu religion.

But why do we chant? The rhythmic repeating of words or sounds relaxes our brains, centers our energies, and raises our consciousness when we chant. This shift in consciousness enables us to access higher levels of awareness, where we can have remarkable experiences of clarity, insight, calm, and connection.

Chanting also has a vibrational power. Because everything in the cosmos, including us, is made up of energy vibrating at different frequencies, the sound vibrations produced while chanting have the potential to modify our physical and subtle bodies.

It is entirely up to you whether you engage in prayer, chanting, both, or none. Remember that there are numerous paths to the divine, and yours is unique to you. What's important is that your chosen route is real to you and brings you to deeper love, calm, and connection.

I welcome you to try these practices as you continue to explore and progress on your spiritual journey. They can be a lovely addition to your spiritual toolkit, expanding your heart, soothing your mind, and connecting you to the universe. Be gentle with yourself, have an open mind to new experiences, and remember that the journey is just as essential as the destination.

5.3 The Role of Nature in Spirituality

Nature is an amazing orchestra that makes the music of the world. It's a never-ending canvas that shows the wonder of life in colors that are both beautiful and simple. Nature has a special place in faith because of how wise and beautiful it is.

In the business of modern life, it can be easy to forget that we are a natural part of the world. We are not different or better than anything else. Instead, we are all tied together in a magical dance of life with every tree, mountain, river, animal, breeze, and sunset. This is a very humbling and awe-inspiring discovery.

When we spend time in nature, we get back in touch with our roots and with what it means to be living. We can see the cycles of life – birth, growth, death, and rebirth – in the way the seasons change, the moon grows and shrinks, and the waves rise and fall.

When we walk barefoot on the grass and feel the ground beneath us, we bond with the Earth's energy. When we feel the sun's warmth on our skin, we connect with its life-giving force. When we listen to the leaves rustling, the birds singing, and the wind whispering, we hear the music of life.

Nature can be a strong mirror that shows us what is going on inside of us. The peace we feel inside can be seen in the quiet of a lake. The way a tree stands tall in a storm can show how strong we are on the inside. The vastness of the night sky full of stars can show how much we can do.

Nature can also teach us a lot. It teaches us about change and how things don't last, about being patient and not giving up, about harmony and balance, and about how everything is linked. It reminds us of the rule of cause and effect, which says that every choice and action influences the web of life. It asks us to live in a way that is kind and polite, not just to ourselves and others, but to all living things.

Spending time in nature can also help calm, heal, and reenergize our minds, bodies, and souls. It helps us slow down, relax, and tune out the noise of the outside world so we can tune into the quiet of the inside world. It opens our hearts, minds, and senses, letting us have times of awe, wonder, joy, and connection.

So, how can we use nature as part of our spiritual practices? It could be as easy as taking a mindful walk in a park, meditating under a tree, doing yoga on the beach, gardening, or watching birds. It could be as deep as going on a pilgrimage to a sacred place in nature or taking part in a ceremony or rite that involves nature.

As you keep going on your spiritual path, I ask you to think about how nature fits into your spiritual life. Let nature be your refuge, your teacher, and your reflection zone. Connect with nature, learn from nature, and treat nature with respect. Let nature's wisdom and beauty guide you on your spiritual road.

May you always remember that you are a child of the Earth and the Universe as you dance through life. You are as bright as the sun, as beautiful as the mountains, as big as the ocean, as strong as a tree, and as amazing as a flower in full bloom. Accept this truth, live this wisdom, and let your spirit soar in nature's embrace.

PART III: SPIRITUALITY IN EVERYDAY LIFE

CHAPTER 6: IMPLEMENTING SPIRITUALITY DAILY

*6.1 Integrating Spirituality
in Your Everyday Life*

Spirituality is like a bright thread that ties us to our deepest selves, to others, to the world around us, and to the divine. This thread is woven into the big picture of life. And it's not just a thread for special events; it can be woven into our everyday lives as well. Bringing spirituality into your everyday life doesn't have to be hard, but it does take a clear goal and regular practice. Here are some ways you can bring faith into your everyday life.

Start Your Day With a Plan

A meaningful way to start the day can set the tone for the rest of the day. It could be as simple as taking a few moments after waking up to set a positive goal, express gratitude, or do a mindfulness practice like meditation or deep breathing. This small thing can make a big difference, giving you a sense of calm, focus, and happiness to start your day.

Thoughtful Times

Every day, we have a lot of ordinary moments that, with a little bit of attention, can be turned into special times of connection and awareness. Any moment can be a mindful moment, whether you're enjoying your morning coffee, washing the dishes, going to work, or waiting in line. It's about being fully present in the moment, tuning into your senses, and enjoying the beauty and wonder of the everyday.

Keeping a Spiritual Journal

Keeping a spiritual journal can help you get in touch with your inner world in a strong way. It could be a place for you to share your ideas, feelings, dreams, insights, and experiences. It could be a place where you can think about your spiritual journey, how you've grown, and how you've changed. It's a picture of your inner self and a friend who helps you explore your spirituality.

Kindness Acts

Spirituality isn't just about finding out more about yourself. It's also about seeing how we're all linked and showing that through compassion and kindness. No matter how big or small, acts of kindness are a beautiful way to show our spiritual side. It could be something as easy as a smile, a kind word, or a hand. Every good deed sends out waves of love and happiness into the world.

Nature Connection

As we talked about in the last chapter, nature is a big part of faith. Even if you only have a few minutes a day to connect with nature, this can help your spiritual life. It could be a walk in a park, watching the sun rise or set, or just enjoying a flower in bloom. Let nature touch your mind, heal your heart, and feed your soul.

Gratitude Practice

Practicing gratitude is a strong spiritual practice that can change your view from one of lack to one of abundance and from one of sadness to one of joy. Having a daily gratitude exercise, like writing down the things you're thankful for at the end of the day, can bring more happiness and satisfaction into your life.

Caring for Your Temple

Your body is a shrine where your spirit lives. Taking care of your body by feeding it well, exercising regularly, getting enough rest, and taking care of yourself is a spiritual practice in and of itself. It's about giving respect to the divine in you.

Consuming With Care

A big part of living a spiritual life is being aware of what we take in, like food, media, knowledge, and energy. It's about making decisions that nourish our bodies, minds, and spirits and are in line with our values and our connection to all life.

At first, it might be hard to fit these routines into your daily life, and that's fine. Remember, change doesn't happen overnight. It takes time to change how you do things. So, give yourself some time. Start by taking baby steps. Celebrate your progress. And most important, have fun on the way.

Every day is a chance to weave faith into your life, to give meaning and magic to your everyday moments, and to live in line with your deepest truth. And as you do this, you will see a big change. There will be more peace, joy, love, and unity in your life. You will become more aware, more kind, more rooted, and stronger. And you'll understand that spirituality isn't just something you do at certain times or in certain places. It's something you live, breathe, and show every day.

6.2 Spiritual Rituals and Routines

Spiritual practices and habits are like the heartbeat of our spiritual practice. They pulse with the rhythm of the sacred and give consistency and depth to our spiritual journey. Rituals and routines can help us connect our everyday life to our spiritual life by keeping us in the present. They can turn ordinary moments into times of connection, awareness, and respect.

Meditation Every Day

Setting up a daily meditation practice can be a life-changing habit. It doesn't matter if you relax for 5 minutes or 50 minutes as long as you do it regularly. Choose a time that works best for you, find a quiet place to reflect, and try to do it at the same time every day. Over time, the relaxing and focusing effects of meditation will start to show up in other parts of your life.

Mornings with Thought

A good day can start with a good practice in the morning. You might want to start your day with a few mindful activities, like deep breathing, yoga, writing in a book, or praying. A walk in the woods can also help you feel better when you wake up. When you wake up and spend time on your faith, it gives you a deep sense of peace and helps you stay focused all day.

Holy Ground

Creating a sacred place in your home can help you with your spiritual rituals. This could be a small spot where you pray, think, or relax. Decorate it with things that inspire you emotionally, like candles, crystals, spiritual texts, photos of spiritual leaders, or natural elements. If you come back to this place every day, it can help you feel more connected to your spiritual practice.

Spiritual Reading

Set aside some time every day to read spiritual works or books that lift you up. You can do this in the morning or before bed. The words and knowledge in these readings can help you on your spiritual journey by giving you direction, insight, and food.

Gratitude Ritual

Make it a habit to say "thank you" every day. This could be done by keeping a gratitude book, saying a prayer of thanks before meals, or just taking a few minutes to think about what you're grateful for. This ritual can help you focus on the good things in your life, making you feel happy and satisfied.

Nightly Thoughts

Take some time to think about your day before you go to sleep. Recognize your successes, the lessons you've learned, the joys you've had, and the problems you've had to deal with. This thought can help you wrap up your day and feel more at peace with yourself and the world.

Digital Detox

In this age of electronics, taking a break from them can be a spiritually refreshing and reviving practice. You could set aside a certain amount of time each day, like the first hour after you wake up or the last hour before you go to bed, when you don't use any devices. Use this time for spiritual activities or just to get in touch with yourself and your surroundings.

<u>Silence as a Ritual</u>

Make quiet time a regular part of your routine. This could be a few minutes of silence every day, or it could be a day of the week when you stay quiet for a longer time. Silence gives us a chance to listen to our inner knowledge and makes us feel calm and clear.

Remember that the point of these practices and habits is not to give you more things to do, but to give you sacred moments in your everyday life. Change them to fit your needs and way of life. Don't worry if you miss one or two days. What counts is that you try.

By doing these things every day, you'll slowly develop a spiritual pace that fits your inner self. You'll find that your days are easier and more graceful, and that you're more aware of the spiritual parts of your life. So, let these practices and habits be your daily anchors that keep you in the present and bring you closer to the spiritual world.

6.3 Spirituality in Work and Play

Spirituality is not confined to specific practices or moments; it permeates every aspect of our life, including our work and leisure activities. It's about bringing the essence of our spiritual self – our authenticity, presence, and compassion – into every situation. When we infuse our work and play with spirituality, we transform these experiences into opportunities for growth, connection, and fulfillment. Here's how you can weave the threads of spirituality into your work and leisure activities.

Spirituality in Work

Intention

Start your workday by setting a positive intention. It could be an intention to stay focused, to be kind and patient, or to do your best. This simple act can bring a sense of purpose and mindfulness to your work.

Mindfulness

Practice mindfulness at work. This means being fully present in what you're doing, whether it's writing a report, attending a meeting, or interacting with a colleague. It's about engaging in each task with full attention and openness. Mindfulness can enhance your performance, reduce stress, and bring a deeper sense of fulfillment to your work.

Purpose

Connect your work with a greater purpose. Regardless of what your job is, it's contributing to something bigger. Maybe it's helping a business grow, providing a service to others, or creating something of value. Recognizing this purpose can bring a spiritual dimension to your work.

Compassion

Bring compassion into your workplace. Show kindness and understanding to your colleagues, listen to their perspectives, and support them when they're facing challenges. Compassion not only fosters a positive work environment but also resonates with our spiritual values of interconnectedness and love.

Balance

Maintain a healthy work-life balance. It's easy to get caught up in the demands of work but remember that rest and recreation are equally important for your well-being and spiritual growth. Prioritize self-care and make time for spiritual practices.

Spirituality in Play

Joy

Engage in activities that bring you joy. Joy is a high-vibration emotion that aligns us with our spiritual nature. It could be a hobby, a sport, a creative pursuit, or simply playing with your pet. Let your heart lead you to your joy.

Nature

Spend leisure time in nature. As we discussed in previous chapters, nature is a potent source of spiritual nourishment. Whether it's a hike in the woods, a stroll on the beach, or gardening in your backyard, connecting with nature can be a deeply spiritual experience.

Presence

Be fully present in your leisure activities. Whether you're reading a book, painting, or playing a game, immerse yourself in the activity. Let go of the past and future, and savor the joy of the present moment.

Creativity

Tap into your creativity. Creativity is a powerful form of self-expression and a channel for spiritual exploration. It could be through art, writing, music, dance, or any form that resonates with you. When you create from your heart, you connect with the divine creative energy within you.

Connection

Use your leisure time to connect with others. Social interactions – whether it's playing a game, having a meaningful conversation, or sharing a meal – can be opportunities for spiritual connection. They remind us of our shared humanity and our inherent interconnectedness.

Infusing spirituality into your work and play doesn't require any drastic changes. It's about shifting your perspective, bringing mindfulness and heartfulness into your actions, and recognizing the spiritual opportunities in your everyday experiences. As you do this, you'll find that your work becomes a medium for your spiritual expression and your play becomes a celebration of your spiritual essence. So, let your work and play reflect the light of your spirit, and let your spirit be nourished by the joy and fulfillment of your work and play.

CHAPTER 7: SPIRITUALITY AND MENTAL HEALTH

7.1 The Link Between Spirituality and Mental Health

There is a deep and complicated link between spirituality and mental health. Our spiritual health has a big effect on our mental health, and our mental health can also influence our spiritual experience. This link is supported by a lot of study, personal stories, and the experiences of a lot of people. It's a connection that deserves to be investigated and understood.

Spirituality gives us a framework for knowing who we are, where we fit in the world, and how we are connected to other people and the universe. It answers the big questions we all have about life, giving us a sense of meaning, belonging, and hope. These things are important for a good mental state because they give us a sense of worth and help us deal with life's problems with optimism and resilience.

<u>Spirituality as a Comfort and Strength Source</u>

There is a lot of doubt, change, and trouble in life. A lot of people find comfort and strength in their spiritual views and practices during times of trouble. Spirituality can give people a comforting view that helps them make sense of their lives, see their problems in a bigger picture, and keep hope for the future. This source of inner strength and grit can help protect mental health in a big way.

The Power of Spiritual Practices to Heal

Meditation, prayer, mindfulness, and rituals are all spiritual activities that have been shown to be good for mental health. Mindfulness and meditation, for example, have been shown to help lower stress, anxiety, and depression, as well as improve attention and emotional control. They help us connect with our inner peace and make us feel calm and balanced. These activities also make room for self-reflection and self-awareness, which are important for mental health.

Spirituality and Help from Others

Whether it's a religious gathering, a meditation group, or a spiritual retreat, spirituality often involves a sense of community. This social part gives you a network of support, which can be very good for your mental health. It gives people a feeling of belonging, a chance to make meaningful connections, and help when things are hard.

Why and What It Means

Having a feeling of purpose and meaning in life is an important part of having a healthy mind. Spirituality, which looks at life, can often do this. It gives people a feeling of direction, encourages them to work for a greater good, and puts their life experiences in a bigger picture. This feeling of purpose and meaning can boost self-esteem, make life more enjoyable, and improve mental health.

Self-Surpassing and Being Kind

Self-transcendence is an important part of many spiritual traditions and practices. It means going beyond our individual selves to link with a bigger whole. This way of thinking can help people feel more empathy, kindness, and altruism, which are all good for mental health. Having empathy and care for others can make you feel less alone, improve your relationships, and make you feel more fulfilled.

It's important to keep in mind that the connection between faith and mental health is very individual and can be very different for each person. Some people find comfort and strength in their faith, while for others, it may not be as important. The important thing is to recognize and accept that different people have different experiences and to think of spirituality as one of many tools we can use to improve our mental health and well-being. Spirituality, at its core, pushes us to accept ourselves as whole, to work on finding inner peace, and to connect with the whole of life. By doing these things, it helps our mental health.

7.2 Spirituality as a Tool for Stress Management

Stress is something we all must deal with. It can be caused by things like stress at work, problems with relationships, worries about health, or just the fast pace of modern life. But even though we can't stop stress, how we deal with it makes a big difference in how it affects our lives. Here is where faith can be a transformative tool by giving people a place to rest and a way to keep going.

Making Peace with Yourself

At its core, faith helps people feel calm and at peace with themselves. This peace doesn't depend on what's going on outside of us; it comes from inside of us. Regular spiritual practices like meditation, prayer, or being aware of the present moment help build this inner peace, which is like an anchor in a sea of worry. This calm, grounded place is our safe place, where stress melts away and the mind gets clear and focused again.

Building Strength

Spirituality also helps us get through hard times. It gives us a sense of purpose and direction that helps us deal with the ups and downs of life. Believing in a bigger cosmic order or a higher power can give us comfort and strength when we're going through hard times. It can help us see our problems as temporary obstacles instead of impossible ones.

Fostering Mindfulness

Mindfulness is a key part of many spiritual practices and a powerful way to deal with stress. By putting all our attention on the present, we can stop worrying about the past or the future, which can make us feel stressed. We also learn to pay more attention to our bodies, which helps us notice signs of stress early on, before they get out of hand.

Helping People Accept

A lot of spiritual ideas stress the power of acceptance. We learn to accept things as they are, instead of trying to change them or acting on impulse. This doesn't mean we have to give in to stress, but rather that we must accept it as a part of our lives right now. This acceptance can lessen the strong feelings that often come with stress, making it easier to deal with the problem in a calm and effective way.

Getting in Touch with Nature

For many people, being spiritual means having a close relationship with nature. Spending time in nature can lower stress, help you relax, and make you feel better. Getting close to nature, whether it's through a walk in the park, gardening, or just watching the sun set, can be very healing.

Taking Care of Yourself

Spirituality reminds us of how important it is to take care of our minds, bodies, and spirits. This can be done in many ways, like getting enough sleep, eating well, being active, doing relaxation techniques, or doing things we love. By putting ourselves first, we improve our ability to deal with stress.

Remember that spirituality is a process that is different for everyone. What works for one person might not work for another. It's about figuring out what makes you feel good and putting those things into your life. So, look into, try out, and use the spiritual tools that will help you handle stress with grace and strength. You can get away from stress and find peace and strength in the spiritual refuge inside of you.

7.3 Fostering Positivity Through Spiritual Practices

Spiritual practices are like gateways to a reservoir of positivity and joy within us. They connect us to our deepest essence and help us see the world with a fresh, appreciative gaze. These practices, whether they are meditation, prayer, mindfulness, or rituals, offer unique ways to cultivate positivity and uplift our spirits.

Meditation and Mindfulness

Meditation and mindfulness practices invite us to step away from the clamor of external distractions and tune into the quietude within us. Here, we can witness the ebb and flow of our thoughts without getting entangled in them. This peaceful detachment helps us cultivate a positive mindset. We realize that our thoughts are transient, and we have the power to choose positivity over negativity. Moreover, these practices ground us in the present moment, where we can appreciate the simple joys that we often overlook.

Gratitude Practice

Gratitude is a deeply spiritual practice that can drastically shift our focus from what's wrong in our lives to what's right. Whether it's maintaining a gratitude journal or simply taking a few moments each day to count our blessings, these acts of thankfulness generate a wave of positivity. They make us realize the abundance that already exists in our lives, fostering contentment and joy.

Prayer and Affirmations

Prayer, in various forms, is a fundamental part of many spiritual traditions. It offers a way to communicate with a higher power, express our hopes and fears, and seek guidance. The process of prayer can be incredibly comforting and uplifting, filling us with positivity. Similarly, affirmations, or positive statements about ourselves and our lives, can alter our mindset. They serve as reminders of our worth, our capabilities, and the potential for good in our lives.

Nature Connection

Connecting with nature is another spiritual practice that fosters positivity. The beauty and tranquility of nature can evoke feelings of awe and wonder, putting our individual worries into perspective. Being in nature can reduce stress, increase our mood, and cultivate a sense of inner peace. It can remind us of the simple pleasures in life and the interconnectedness of all beings.

Acts of Kindness and Service

Performing acts of kindness and service can be a deeply spiritual practice, fostering positivity in multiple ways. It not only makes us feel good about ourselves but also strengthens our sense of connection with others. Knowing that we've made a difference, however small, can light up our spirits. It underscores the idea that our lives have purpose and meaning beyond our individual needs and desires.

Yoga and Movement

Yoga and other forms of movement can be spiritual practices that boost positivity. They help us connect with our bodies, release pent-up emotions, and generate feel-good hormones. Yoga with its emphasis on breath and alignment, fosters a sense of harmony between our bodies, minds, and spirits.

Through consistent practice, these spiritual practices foster positivity that extends beyond the practice itself. They help us cultivate a positive, spiritual mindset that permeates our lives, enabling us to navigate life's challenges with more ease, resilience, and joy. Embrace these practices with an open heart, and watch as your life blossoms with positivity.

CHAPTER 8: SPIRITUALITY AND RELATIONSHIPS

8.1 Cultivating Spiritual Bonds

There is more to a relationship than merely an emotional or physical connection between two people. They present a chance for personal development and evolution on a spiritual level, serving as a mirror that reflects our own inner reality. When two people share a spiritual connection with one another, it indicates that their relationship has evolved to a more profound level, one in which they acknowledge and respect the presence of the divine in the other. The following are some ways in which we can strengthen the spiritual links that exist inside our relationships.

<u>Being Present While Mindful</u>

Being completely present in the moments you share with others is the bedrock of a spiritual connection. It involves giving the other person your undivided attention while listening and picking up on their feelings and requirements without being distracted. This kind of conscious presence is becoming an increasingly rare gift in today's fast-paced and digitalized world. Maintain an attentive attitude in all your interactions. Put away your electronic distractions, make eye contact with the person you're speaking with, and listen not just with your ears but also with your heart. A spiritual connection can be fostered through the kind of in-depth listening that also involves empathy.

Compassion and awareness of others' perspectives

The capacity to comprehend and empathize with the anguish and challenges experienced by another person is what we mean when we talk about compassion. When two people share a spiritual connection, compassion develops into an automatic response. It is necessary to delve deeper than the behaviors on the surface in order to comprehend the buried hurts or concerns. This enhanced comprehension helps to cultivate compassion and forgiveness, transforming disagreements into chances for greater connection and personal development.

Authenticity and a Willingness to Be Vulnerable

You must bring your authentic self into the relationship if you want to create a spiritual connection between the two of you. It's about letting go of the masks and the pretenses you put on and embracing your true self so that you can be recognized and loved. Authenticity requires exposing some degree of vulnerability. It requires exposing your vulnerabilities, such as your anxieties, your dreams, and your insecurities, and opening your heart to others. It is about being willing to declare, "This is who I am, in all of my imperfections, and I allow you to see me." A genuine and exposed display of vulnerability is the seed that grows a strong spiritual connection.

Priorities and Core Values in Common

A spiritual connection is frequently founded on a set of shared beliefs and ideals. These values could include a dedication to personal development, a love for the natural world, a search for the truth, or an appreciation for the outdoors. They promote a sense of unity and purpose in the relationship, acting as a guiding compass for the partnership as a whole. The spiritual connection can also be strengthened through engaging in shared spiritual practices, such as meditation or prayer.

Unconditional Love

The ability to love without conditions is the driving force behind all spiritual connections. This is the kind of love that is independent of any prerequisites. It is not about trying to change or exert control over the other person but rather embracing and loving them in their current state. It is a love that is unshakeable despite the ups and downs that life throws at it, a love that recognizes and respects the divine nature that is within the other person.

Developing spiritual connections isn't always a walk in the park. To get beyond the superficial levels of connection, one must have a certain amount of self-awareness, as well as commitment and guts. However, the benefits are tremendous. A spiritual connection has the power to change a relationship into a holy space that can be used for personal development, healing, and love. This is the kind of place where two souls can meet and recognize each other in their most fundamental form.

8.2 The Power of Forgiveness

Forgiveness is the salve that heals wounds and mends ties in the world of relationships. People often think that forgiving someone means you agree with what they did that hurt you, but in fact, forgiving is a deep spiritual practice that frees the forgiver more than anyone else.

Understanding Forgiveness

In the end, forgiveness is about letting go of the toxic weight of bitterness, anger, or revenge that we carry inside us. It's about being aware of the pain we've been through but deciding to let go of the bad feelings that keep us tied to that pain. It's a choice to go on with more understanding, kindness, and strength.

The Importantance to Forgive Spiritually

From a spiritual point of view, forgiveness shows how strong love is and how temporary mistakes are. It is realizing that we are all divine beings on a human journey, and that sometimes we stumble. But our mistakes don't make us or the people who hurt us who they are.

When we forgive, we admit that this is true. We're getting past the mistake and realizing that each of us has a divine part. We've decided to choose love over anger, and understanding over revenge.

Learning to Forgive

It's not always easy to forget, especially when our pain is real and deep. Keep in mind that forgiving someone is a process, not a one-time thing. It all starts with being ready to forgive.

Start by letting yourself feel your pain and letting yourself heal. Try to have understanding for other people, and figure out why they do what they do. Like us, they are formed by what they have done, what they fear, and what they can't do.

Meditation and prayer are spiritual activities that can help you feel more peaceful and caring inside. Do things to help you forgive, like writing a letter of forgiveness that you don't have to send, or imagining letting go of the person who hurt you.

The Power of Letting Go

Forgiveness is a strong thing. It doesn't change what happened, but it can change how you think about what happened. It gets rid of anger in your heart, making room for love and joy. It gives you peace and lets you out of the cage of old hurts.

It also makes ways for people to get along. In relationships, it lets us start over with a clean slate, which helps us understand and accept each other more. Even when it's not possible or good to make up, forgiveness lets you move on without carrying around the weight of resentment.

In terms of spiritual growth, forgiveness is the key to personal freedom. It raises our awareness and brings us closer to our real, divine nature, which is a state of boundless love and compassion. Accept the power of forgiveness and see how it changes your relationships for the better.

8.3 Expressing Love and Compassion

Spirituality is all about love and compassion, which come from the idea that we are all linked at the deepest level. In partnerships, these traits can strengthen bonds, help people understand each other, and make everyone feel better.

How to Understand Love and Kindness

Love in a spiritual sense goes beyond sexual love or love between family members. It is a positive regard for others that doesn't depend on them doing anything. It means recognizing their natural worth and honoring their divine essence. This love doesn't depend on what the other person does, how they act, or what they are like; it's a way of being that affects everything we do.

On the other hand, compassion is a reaction of empathy to the suffering of others, along with a desire to make that suffering go away. It's about putting ourselves in someone else's place and feeling what they feel, without losing ourselves in the process.

How Love and Kindness Play a Part in Relationships

When people in a partnership show love and care for each other, it makes it safe for them to connect in a real way. It motivates people to be open and vulnerable, which are two things that are needed for deep, meaningful relationships. Love and compassion help people accept and understand each other, which makes it easier to deal with conflicts and disagreements.

Putting Love and Compassion into Action

The first step in showing love and kindness is to love and care for yourself. When we develop a loving relationship with ourselves, we are better able to show this love to others.

Mindfulness: Being mindful helps us stay in the moment and connect with ourselves and other people. It helps us listen more carefully, learn better, and show our love and care in a more genuine way.

Kindness: Every day, do small acts of kindness. Kind words, real compliments, and lending a hand are all ways to show that you care.

Try to understand how other people think and feel without passing judgment. Empathy makes us more compassionate and helps us act in a thoughtful and helpful way.

As we've already talked about, forgiving someone is a strong way to show love and compassion. It shows that you are willing to move on from mistakes and see the value in others.

Showing thanks often can make it easier for you to love. When you appreciate other people and recognize what they've done for you, you strengthen your relationships with them.

How Love and Compassion Can Make a Difference

The way you show love and care can change your relationships and how you feel about life. It can heal old scars, bring people together, and make them feel like they belong. It makes for happiness, peace, and growth for everyone. By showing love and compassion, you not only make other people feel better, but you also feed your own spirit. This brings you closer to the spiritual truth that we are all linked and one.

PART IV: CHALLENGES AND GROWTH

CHAPTER 9: OVERCOMING SPIRITUAL OBSTACLES

9.1 Understanding Common Spiritual Challenges

Every spiritual journey has its dark nights of the soul, or hard times. These problems are not roadblocks, but rather stepping stones that help us learn more about ourselves and grow spiritually. Let's talk about some common spiritual challenges that people on this path might face and how knowing them can help us get through them better.

Uncertainty and Doubt

Doubt is something that many people face on their spiritual path. This can look like doubt about spiritual practices or ideas, or even doubting one's own experiences. Doubt, on the other hand, is not inherently bad. It can lead to more research, making us question, test, and prove our views instead of blindly accepting them.

Loneliness and Misunderstanding

Spiritual growth can be a lonely process at times, especially if the people around us don't share our beliefs or experiences. We might feel like no one gets us or that we don't belong. It's important to keep in mind that it's okay to go your own way and that there are groups and tools out there where you can find people who are like you.

Opposition and Fear

Even good changes can be scary. As we start to grow mentally, we might meet resistance from ourselves or others. We can be held back by fear of the unknown, fear of losing control, or fear of how other people will respond. We can get past these fears by recognizing them and realizing that they are a normal part of the process.

Restlessness and Anger

Spiritual growth is not a goal; it is a process that lasts a lifetime. But we are often anxious and want answers or knowledge right away. This impatience can make things worse and make people lose hope. It's important to know that spiritual growth takes time and care, just like how a seed grows into a tree.

The Trap of Ego

As we move forward on our spiritual path, there is a chance that we will fall into the "ego trap". This means that we will become too attached to our spiritual achievements or start to think that we are "more enlightened" than other people. This is just the ego trying to look holy. For real spiritual progress, it's important to stay humble and be aware of the ego trap.

The first step to solving these problems is to know what they are. They are not signs of failure, but rather invitations to strengthen our spiritual practice by practicing patience, understanding, and compassion. Rumi said, "The wound is the place where the Light enters you." In the same way, these problems can be ways for more spiritual light to come into our lives.

9.2 Strategies for Overcoming Obstacles

Addressing spiritual challenges requires a combination of self-awareness, resilience, and a toolbox of strategies to navigate the bumps along the journey. Here are several strategies that can help.

Embrace the Journey

Recognize that challenges are part of the spiritual path, not detours. They are opportunities for growth and self-discovery. Rather than resisting these obstacles, embrace them with curiosity and a willingness to learn.

Cultivate Patience

Spiritual growth is not a race; it's a lifelong journey. Cultivate patience with yourself and the process. Trust that with time, practice, and intention, you'll continue to evolve and grow.

Stay Grounded in the Present Moment

Obstacles often arise when we're either dwelling in the past or worrying about the future. Practice mindfulness to stay grounded in the present moment. Use meditative practices like focusing on your breath or tuning into the sensations in your body to anchor yourself in the now.

Seek Support

Don't hesitate to seek support when you're facing spiritual challenges. This support can come from a spiritual mentor, a supportive community, or therapeutic modalities like counseling or coaching. You're not alone on your journey, and there's no shame in seeking help.

Practice Self-Compassion

Be kind to yourself as you navigate your spiritual path. It's okay to stumble, to doubt, to struggle. Treat yourself with the same compassion and understanding you'd extend to a dear friend facing the same challenges.

Regular Meditation and Reflection

Maintaining a regular practice of meditation can provide a safe space to explore and understand your challenges. Additionally, journaling or self-reflection can help you recognize patterns, process emotions, and gain insights.

Use Affirmations

Affirmations are powerful tools to reprogram negative thought patterns. Develop positive, empowering affirmations to guide you through difficult times. For instance, if you're struggling with impatience, your affirmation might be, "I trust the timing of my life and my spiritual journey."

Stay Open and Flexible

Your spiritual path may not look exactly as you imagined, and that's okay. Stay open to the journey unfolding in unexpected ways. Flexibility can help you adapt and grow in the face of challenges.

Nourish Your Body

The connection between mind and body is profound. Regular exercise, a healthy diet, and sufficient rest can enhance your mental and emotional wellbeing, making it easier to cope with spiritual obstacles.

Connect with Nature

Nature can be a powerful ally in overcoming spiritual challenges. Spending time outdoors can help you feel grounded, present, and connected to something larger than yourself.

Remember, overcoming spiritual obstacles isn't about eradicating all challenges or discomforts from your path. It's about learning to navigate them with grace, resilience, and a sense of growth. These strategies can guide you through the hurdles, illuminating your path towards deeper spiritual awareness.

9.3 The Risk and Reality of Spiritual Bypassing

Spiritual growth and discovery can be hampered by something called "spiritual bypassing." In the 1980s, psychologist John Welwood came up with this term to describe how people use spiritual practices and beliefs to avoid dealing with uncomfortable feelings, unresolved hurts, and basic emotional and psychological needs.

Understanding Spiritual Bypassing

Spiritual skipping is all about getting away from things. It's about using spirituality as a shield or a way to escape from hard feelings or painful situations. This avoidance is often covered up by spiritual practices that seem good, making it harder to see.

For example, you might use techniques like meditation or mantras to stop yourself from feeling angry or sad instead of figuring out why you feel that way. Or you could believe that "everything happens for a reason" to avoid the pain of loss or the discomfort of not knowing why something bad happened.

The Dangers of Skipping Out on God

Spiritual skipping might help you feel better in the short term, but in the long run, it can stop you from growing spiritually and emotionally. This is why:

- *Neglects Emotional Health*: Emotions, even the ones that make us feel bad, are part of being human and can teach us important things. If you don't deal with these feelings or try to hide them, you could end up with unresolved emotional damage and bad mental health.

- *Stops Authentic Growth*: If we want to grow spiritually, we must face our doubts, our fears, and our pain. By avoiding these obstacles, we stay in the same patterns and don't grow as much as we could.

- *Relationship stress:* Relationships can also be put under stress by spiritual ignoring. If we don't tell the truth about how we feel, it can make our interactions less real and close.

- *Can Lead to disappointment*: When spiritual practices used for bypassing don't bring lasting peace or happiness, it can lead to disappointment or a crisis of faith.

Overcoming Spiritual Bypassing

To stop spiritual skipping, you need to be self-aware, honest, and brave. Here are some things you can do to help:

- *Acknowledge Your Feelings*:   Let yourself feel all of your feelings without judging yourself. Know that it's okay to feel angry, sad, scared, or sad.

- *Get help from a professional.* Therapists and counselors who are trained in spiritual problems can help you deal with and get over spiritual bypassing.

- Mindful self-compassion means being kind to yourself as you go through this. It's okay if you find this hard. Self-compassion can help you feel better and help you grow.

- *Integrate your mind, body, and spirit*:   Remember that spiritual growth isn't just about going beyond the physical and mental worlds. It's also about bringing together all the parts of who you are.

Spiritual skipping takes you off the path to real spiritual growth. Seeing it and doing something about it can lead to a deeper and more fulfilling spiritual journey based on truth, honesty, and overall well-being.

CHAPTER 10: CULTIVATING SPIRITUAL RESILIENCE

10.1 Spirituality During Hard Times

Life is a complex tapestry woven with threads of joy, love, loss, and pain. Each of us will encounter challenges and hardships, moments when our spirit feels tested to its limits. Yet, it's precisely during these difficult times that spirituality can become a lighthouse guiding us through the storm. Let's explore how we can lean on spirituality during life's toughest moments.

Facing Life's Storms

Every life journey will have its share of storms. These might be personal challenges, like the loss of a loved one, illness, or job loss. Or they could be collective hardships, like social unrest, environmental crises, or global pandemics. It's during these moments that we might feel our spirit being rocked, our faith being tested. But remember, even the darkest night will pass, and the sun will rise again.

<u>Finding Solace in Spirituality</u>

Spirituality can be a beacon of hope during hard times. It can offer comfort, foster resilience, and provide a broader perspective that goes beyond our immediate circumstances. It can remind us of our innate strength, the interconnectivity of all beings, and the impermanence of all things, including pain and hardship.

Here are some ways to lean into your spirituality during challenging times:

<u>Spiritual Rituals and Practices</u>: Your spiritual practices can become a sanctuary when the outside world feels chaotic or painful. Meditating, praying, journaling, chanting, or spending time in nature can bring solace and perspective.

<u>Embrace the Lessons</u>: Remember that challenges are also opportunities for growth. Ask yourself, "What is this experience teaching me?" You might discover new strengths, develop deeper empathy, or reevaluate what truly matters in life.

<u>Connect with a Spiritual Community</u>: Being part of a spiritual community can provide support and understanding during hard times. Whether it's an organized religious group, a yoga class, or an online spiritual discussion forum, these communities can remind you that you're not alone.

<u>Cultivate Mindfulness</u>: Mindfulness can help us navigate hard times by grounding us in the present moment. It can bring a sense of peace amid chaos and help us respond to challenges with more clarity and equanimity.

<u>Nurture Hope</u>: Spirituality can nurture hope, reminding us of the cyclical nature of life — after every winter, there's a spring. Trust in the process of life and the unfolding journey.

Spirituality during hard times is like a lighthouse in the storm. It doesn't remove the storm, but it illuminates our path, helping us navigate through the rough waters. It reminds us of our inherent strength and resilience, offers comfort and perspective, and encourages us to learn and grow from our challenges.

10.2 Growing Through Adversity

One of the most important things about faith is that it can help us grow, even and especially when things are hard. Even though hard times can shake us to the core, they can also be some of the best teachers. Most of the time, it's in these times that we grow the most spiritually. Here's how we can use a growth mindset to deal with problems and turn them into opportunities for physical and spiritual growth.

<u>The Magic of Hard Times</u>

In the past, alchemists thought it was possible to turn base metals into gold, which is a metaphor for the spiritual journey. Just like the alchemist changes common metal into valuable gold, we can change the hard things that happen to us into knowledge and growth. This process, which is often called "spiritual alchemy," is the journey of turning pain into knowledge and suffering into personal and spiritual growth.

<u>A Path to Spiritual Growth Through Difficult Times</u>

Here are some ways to help people grow through hard times:

Accept the Lessons. Every struggle, no matter how hard it is, has a seed of wisdom inside it. Think to yourself, "What can I learn from this?" What does it teach me about myself, other people, and life in general?" Embracing the lessons that hard times teach us can help us grow and learn more.

Practice acceptance. Fighting against pain or hard times often makes our pain worse. Acceptance doesn't mean we like or approve of the way things are right now. It means we see it for what it is, which is an important first step toward change.

Cultivate compassion. Difficult times can help us open our minds, which makes us more compassionate toward ourselves and others. When we go through hard times, we can better understand the pain of others and feel more connected to them.

Reframe Your View. How we see our problems can have a big effect on how we feel about them. Instead of seeing trouble as a punishment or a problem, you could see it as a chance to grow and learn.

Lean on Your Spiritual Practices. Use the things you do spiritually as tools for change. Meditation, prayer, writing in a book, or spending time in nature are all ways to find peace, gain insights, and heal.

Ask for Help. Don't be afraid to ask for help from friends, family, a spiritual group, or a mental health expert. When we're going through hard times, connection and society can be very helpful.

Remember that bad things don't make you who you are, but how you deal with them can. We find out how strong we are, how resilient we are, how compassionate we are, and how much we grow when we go through hard times. In the alchemical cauldron of life, we have the power to turn trouble into something that helps us grow as people and as spiritual beings. In this way, we don't just stay alive; we also thrive and grow in deep and life-changing ways.

10.3 Maintaining Hope and Positivity

Trying to stay hopeful and positive when things are bad can feel like trying to keep a small lamp lit in a storm. But it's during these times of chaos that the calming effect of faith can be a real lifesaver. It's important to remember that hope and positivity aren't about denying or avoiding problems. Instead, they're about being strong and keeping things in perspective, about accepting the truth of our problems and knowing that storms pass, and the sun always comes back.

Let's look at how faith can act as a lighthouse and lead us to places where we can find hope and positivity.

First, spiritual practices like meditation, prayer, mindfulness, or writing in a gratitude journal on a daily basis can help us stay in the present. These habits can help you create a peaceful place inside yourself that you can go to when things going on outside of you feel too much.

Also, looking at things through a spiritual lens helps us see problems as possibilities. It asks us to think about how each difficulty we face is not a dead end but a fork in the road that can lead to growth, knowledge, and change. This view doesn't make our pain go away, but it does help us see how our struggles fit into the bigger picture of our emotional and spiritual growth.

The power of the mind is a central idea in many spiritual paths, and practicing positive mantras and visualization can have a huge effect. By telling ourselves often that we are strong and resilient and by picturing the good things we want to happen, we can change our minds and make them more open to hope and happiness.

Also, faith often makes us want to connect deeply with the natural world. Spending time in nature, watching its movements, and being amazed by its ability to grow back can remind us of how strong life is. Just like winter always gives way to spring, hard times in our lives give way to times of peace and happiness.

Let's not forget how important self-compassion is in all of these activities. During hard times, we should remember to be our own best friend by letting ourselves feel what we feel without judging ourselves, showing ourselves care and understanding, and reminding ourselves of our worth.

Lastly, you could try to find comfort in a spiritual group. Connecting with people who have the same views and values as you can give you a sense of understanding and community, which can make you feel more hopeful and positive.

PART V: DEEPENING YOUR SPIRITUAL PRACTICE

CHAPTER 11:
ADVANCING IN
SPIRITUAL PRACTICES

*11.1 Deepening Your Meditation
and Mindfulness Practices*

A profound sense of calm can be infused into your life via the use of mindfulness and meditation, which are potent tools that can alter your viewpoint. They give any spiritual practice a solid base. You might want to explore these techniques more thoroughly as you advance on your spiritual path. It is not about adding more time or complexity to your meditation or mindfulness practice; rather, it is about developing a better sense of awareness, presence, and connection.

Let's start by going through your meditation routine. Going beyond passive relaxation and actively interacting with your inner environment are key to deepening your meditation. It involves developing a deeper relationship with your inner self and increasing your awareness of your thoughts, feelings, and bodily sensations. You can do this by gently pushing yourself to remain present even in uncomfortable situations and by examining your feelings with curiosity as opposed to resistance.

You might decide to focus your meditation on harder topics like self-love, acceptance, or forgiveness, for instance. You might also experiment with various meditation techniques, including Vipassana, which promotes a higher degree of introspection and self-awareness. Keep in mind that the objective of meditation is to comprehend and accept whatever comes rather than to reach a certain condition.

Now let's think about how you practice mindfulness. Being completely present in the moment while objectively observing your experiences is what mindfulness is all about. Aim to incorporate this presence into every element of your life in order to increase your mindfulness. Begin to pay attention to the minute elements of your daily activities that you ordinarily ignore, such as the way water feels on your skin after washing your hands or the flavor and texture of your food.

You might also start to practice awareness with your emotions. Practice watching emotions with a sense of detachment rather than responding to them as they occur. Keep track of how they appear in your body and how they change over time. This method can be an effective tool for overcoming emotional obstacles and fostering mental health.

Keep in mind that persistence and patience are essential in your quest to expand your meditation and mindfulness practices. Even though progress could seem slow at times, it's crucial to keep advocating for yourself. You'll probably discover that these techniques eventually result in a stronger sense of inner tranquility, self-awareness, and connectedness to the outside world. This kind of dedication to your practice becomes its own reward, increasing your spiritual path in countless lovely and unanticipated ways.

11.2 Exploring Advanced Techniques and Practices

You can feel the want to broaden your spiritual practices as you continue your path, looking for fresh approaches that will strengthen your ties to the cosmos and yourself. It's a lovely and natural progression that shows how your spiritual life has developed through time. Let's explore some cutting-edge methods and practices that might appeal to you.

Complex Meditation Methods

There are more sophisticated ways that can open new layers of awareness, even though you may have started your meditation journey by concentrating on your breath or physical sensations. There may be uncharted territory worth exploring with meditation practices like transcendental, Kundalini, or Zen. These techniques offer a distinct method to engage your mind and body during meditation since they frequently include features like mantras, visualization, particular breathing patterns, or unusual postures.

Retreats for the soul

A spiritual retreat can offer an immersing experience that significantly accelerates your spiritual development. Such retreats frequently entail long days of mindfulness, meditation, and other spiritual practices, generally in tranquil, natural settings that encourage reflection and peace.

Energy Work

Working with the body's energy systems is the emphasis of techniques like Reiki, Qi Gong, and Tai Chi. Learning to see and control your energy can add a new level to your spiritual practice, increasing your self-awareness and possibly having therapeutic effects.

Spiritual Studies

Your spiritual practice can be improved by developing your grasp of spiritual philosophies, literature, and teachings. You could choose to focus on studying religious texts, reading spiritual leaders' works, or in-depth research on metaphysical ideas.

Mindful Living

This is the process of incorporating awareness into every aspect of your life, from conscious communication to eco-friendly living and mindful eating. It involves coordinating your daily choices and activities with your spiritual principles.

Astral Projection and Lucid Dreaming

These techniques entail raising one's level of awareness when sleeping and dreaming. They can give you tremendous spiritual experiences and deep insights into your unconscious mind.

As you examine these cutting-edge methods and practices, keep in mind to respect each person's unique experience. It's absolutely OK for something to resonate with one individual but not another. The adaptability and uniqueness of spirituality are what make it so beautiful. As you navigate these unfamiliar seas, have an open mind, be observant, and most importantly, be gentle with yourself. It's all a part of your lovely, always changing spiritual path.

11.3 Integrating Rituals for Spiritual Growth

Incorporating rituals into your spiritual practice can provide structure, intentionality, and a sense of sacredness. Rituals help connect us to something larger than ourselves, whether that's the divine, the universe, or the unfolding patterns of nature. They provide touchstones of meaning that can anchor us in our spiritual journey.

While the specifics of a ritual may vary depending on your personal beliefs and spiritual path, the common thread is the intentional repetition of certain actions imbued with symbolic meaning.

<u>Morning and Evening Rituals</u>

Begin and end your day with intention. You might start your morning with meditation, affirmations, or a gratitude practice. Perhaps you choose to drink a glass of water mindfully, connecting with the blessing of clean water and the nourishment it provides. In the evening, you might reflect on the day's experiences, write in a journal, or perform a short meditation before bed. These bookends of your day can provide grounding, perspective, and a consistent touchstone for your spiritual journey.

<u>Rituals of Gratitude</u>

Gratitude is a powerful spiritual practice, and creating a ritual around it can enhance this power. You might keep a gratitude journal, writing down three things you're grateful for each day. Or perhaps you verbally express gratitude before meals, acknowledging the chain of people and processes that brought the food to your table.

Nature Rituals

Connecting with nature can be a potent spiritual practice. You might choose to honor the change of seasons, the full moon, or the solstices and equinoxes with special rituals. This might involve spending time outside, creating a temporary piece of art from natural materials, or reflecting on the symbolic meaning of the season or phase of the moon.

Meditation Rituals

While meditation is a spiritual practice in itself, you can enhance it by creating a ritual around it. This could include lighting a candle or incense, ringing a bell, or saying a prayer or intention before you begin. You might also have a special shawl or blanket you use only for meditation.

Rituals of Release

Sometimes, we need to intentionally let go of things that no longer serve us - whether it's a behavior pattern, a relationship, or a past hurt. A ritual can provide a concrete action to symbolize this internal process. This could involve writing what you want to release on a piece of paper and burning it, or symbolically 'washing away' your old patterns with a special bath.

In creating your rituals, listen to your intuition. What symbols, actions, or practices resonate with you? Remember, these rituals are for you. They should feel meaningful and powerful to you. Over time, your rituals will become an integral part of your spiritual practice, providing familiar touchstones of connection, growth, and depth.

CHAPTER 12: THE ROLE OF DISCIPLINE IN SPIRITUAL GROWTH

12.1 Developing Consistency in Spiritual Practices

Consistency is one of the cornerstones to spiritual progress. It's more important to consistently engage in your spiritual practice than it is to have great, earth-shattering experiences. The real magic is found in this steadiness. But as we are all aware, keeping consistency may occasionally be difficult. Here are some helpful techniques.

Recognizing the Value of Consistency

It's imperative to comprehend the value of consistency before talking about how to cultivate it. We add a brick to the wall of our spiritual life every time we engage in a spiritual activity. That foundation gets stronger the more frequently we turn up. Like our physical muscles, our spiritual muscles get stronger with continued use.

Having Specific Intentions

Be clear about the goals you have for your spiritual practice. Is it mental calmness, a deeper relationship with the cosmos, improved self-awareness, or something else? You will have a concrete reason to continue practicing if you have a defined objective in mind.

Establishing a Routine

It can be quite beneficial to include your spiritual practices into a daily schedule. For instance, you might decide to meditate first thing in the morning or engage in acts of appreciation while taking a break for lunch. Find what suits you the best, then stay with it.

Beginning Small

Start off slowly if you've never engaged in regular spiritual practice. It is preferable to practice daily meditation for five minutes as opposed to once a week for an hour. You can gradually lengthen and intensify your routines as your spiritual muscles develop.

Supporting Flexibility

While maintaining consistency is crucial, flexibility is as necessary. Your usual practice might not be possible on some days. That's alright. Do what you can, and keep in mind that every little bit helps.

Maintaining a Journal

Keeping a journal of your spiritual development might support your routines. Making a record of your learnings, discoveries, and advancements can inspire you and give you a means to monitor your development over time.

Self-Compassion Training

Keep in mind that it's normal to experience ups and downs on your spiritual path. You will experience both days of intense connection and days of disconnection. On the challenging days, be kind to yourself and remember that they are only a part of the trip and not an indication of failure.

It's important to keep in mind that gaining consistency in your spiritual practices is a journey in and of itself, and it's completely normal to encounter obstacles. Keep showing up, be gentle with yourself, and have faith in the spiritual journey you are on.

12.2 Overcoming Challenges in Maintaining Discipline

Keeping up with your spiritual practices on a consistent basis might be difficult at times, yet doing so is not only necessary but also an essential part of your spiritual path. Although approaching these activities with a sense of commitment is crucial, it is also important to identify and work through any problems that may appear along the way. The following is a list of methods that can assist you in overcoming these obstacles:

Recognizing the Challenges, You Face

It is necessary for us to first comprehend the nature of the obstacles standing in our way before we can hope to conquer them. Is there simply not enough time? Motivation on the wane? Distractions? You can begin to directly address individual challenges once you have identified them and categorized them.

Developing a Reliable Behavior Pattern

When it comes to maintaining one's self-discipline, having a regular pattern that one follows on a continuous basis can provide structure and predictability, which can be of great assistance. Set regular times aside for the spiritual activities that are important to you and be sure to honor those commitments. This can help integrate these practices into your daily life and make them feel less like optional activities and more like vital elements of your day as they become more ingrained in your routine.

Seeking Support

You don't have to travel this spiritual path by yourself if you don't want to. You might want to investigate joining a spiritual community or finding a guide who can offer you advice and assistance. This might be a trusted friend who likewise places a high emphasis on spiritual development, a local meditation group, or a community of like-minded people that gather online.

Having Expectations That Are Realistic

It is essential to keep in mind that spiritual development is a process rather than an end goal in and of itself. There is a possibility that there will be periods of rapid advancement, followed by periods of either stagnation or even regress. Don't let the ups and downs of the situation get to you. Instead, you should aim for outcomes that are attainable, and you should continue to attend your practices.

Including a Focus on Mindfulness

Practicing mindfulness throughout our spiritual rituals can assist us in maintaining concentration and being fully present in the moment. Make an effort to bring your attention back to the here and now rather than allowing it to wander off into other ideas or distractions. Your connection to your practices can get stronger as a result, and they can also become more joyful and satisfying for you.

Putting Self-Compassion into Practice

On this path of spiritual discipline, it is absolutely necessary to be kind and compassionate to yourself. Keep in mind that encountering difficulties is a natural part of life, and that any step forward, no matter how tiny, constitutes progress. Self-compassion is a practice that should be adopted, and you should celebrate your efforts in addition to your achievements.

Making Changes to Your Method

It is acceptable to modify an approach that you have been following if you find that it is not producing the desired results for you. Your spiritual journey is one of a kind, and it is essential that you identify practices that ring true for you and are compatible with the way you live your life.

The journey toward sustaining discipline in the spiritual practices you engage in is one that is specific to you. It's quite fine if something that works for one individual doesn't produce the same results for another person. The important thing is to keep your commitment, keep your mind and heart open to new experiences and growth, and treat yourself kindly along the way.

12.3 Strategies for Keeping Your

Spiritual Commitment Alive

It takes regular caring and nurturing to keep the delicate spark of spiritual commitment burning strong. This is a process that takes time to develop; it's a trip that calls for endurance, patience, and willpower. The following tactics can help you maintain your spiritual commitment:

Accept Your 'Why'

Understanding your motivation for embarking on a spiritual path will help you stay more resolute, especially under trying circumstances. Embracing your "why" can inspire you to persevere, whether you're looking for inner peace, a better understanding of the cosmos, or a connection with your higher self.

Create a Daily Routine

Establishing a daily spiritual practice, such as yoga, meditation, or any other form of spiritual exercise, can help you stay committed. It can provide you a sense of order and consistency and acts as a reminder of your spiritual path.

Establish a Sacred Space

Having a location set apart for your spiritual activities will help you concentrate better and strengthen your connection. This doesn't necessarily imply that you require a complete room; even a little area can be turned into a peaceful haven. You can decorate this area with objects that uplift your spirit, such as candles, crystals, spiritual books, or pictures.

Continue to Learn

It's essential to preserve an open mind and a desire to

discover new things if you want to maintain your spiritual devotion. Be open to learning about brand-new spiritual disciplines, theories, and teachings. Keep asking questions and let your spiritual awareness grow.

Find a Spiritual Community to Join

Your sense of belonging and understanding can be further strengthened by interacting with others who share your beliefs. It doesn't matter if this community is found online, on a spiritual retreat, or in a local group; what matters is the mutual support and shared experiences.

Develop Your Gratitude

By keeping you focused on the here and now and allowing you to appreciate the riches in your life, cultivating a sense of gratitude can help you stay committed to your spiritual practice. Think about keeping a thankfulness journal where you can routinely list things for which you are thankful.

Put Self-Care First

Keep in mind that taking care of your general welfare is part of your spiritual commitment. The energy levels required for your spiritual practices can be maintained with regular rest, a healthy diet, and exercise.

Decide to be Persistent and Patient

Finally, keep in mind that the spiritual journey is a marathon, not a sprint. Even while progress might appear to be slow at times, every action—no matter how small—brings you closer to your spiritual objectives. You have two allies in this journey: patience and endurance.

Don't forget that your spiritual path is entirely personal. The methods mentioned above are only recommendations; there is no one way that is the "right" way to maintain your spiritual commitment. Every step you take on your spiritual path is a step towards greater comprehension and connection, so trust your intuition, go with what seems right to you, and follow your heart.

PART VI: A LIFELONG COMMITMENT TO SPIRITUALITY

CHAPTER 13: LIFELONG LEARNING AND GROWTH

13.1 Continuing Education in Spirituality

At its essence, spirituality is a lifelong process of learning and growth. It is about always developing your connection, broadening your awareness, and improving your habits. Continuing education in spirituality, like any other subject of study, can be a rich and satisfying endeavor.

Here's how you can approach lifetime spiritual education:

Make Time for Learning

Set aside regular time for learning, just as you do for meditation or other spiritual disciplines. Reading spiritual writings, listening to spiritual teachers, or attending workshops and retreats could all be part of this.

Broaden Your Horizons

While having a core spiritual practice or tradition is beneficial, don't be afraid to explore others. Studying many spiritual paths can help you gain a more complete view of spirituality and can often improve your primary practice.

Learn from a Variety of Sources

A wealth of materials is accessible to enhance your spiritual growth in today's digital age. Spiritual insights can be gained from books, online courses, podcasts, movies, and even social media platforms.

Find a Spiritual Guide or Mentor

Having a mentor or spiritual guidance can sometimes make or break your spiritual path. Such people can offer tailored advice, answer concerns, offer support through difficult times, and serve as a source of inspiration.

Participate in Group Learning

Learning with others can be quite beneficial. Consider attending workshops and seminars or joining a spiritual study group. The group learning discussions, shared experiences, and collective energy can bring unique insights and expand your comprehension.

Practicing, Reflecting, and Integrating

Continuing education in spirituality is about more than just learning; it's about using that information in your daily life. Take the time to think on new thoughts or practices as you learn them and find ways to incorporate them into your spiritual regimen.

Keep an open mind and a curious mind!

With an open mind and a sense of curiosity, approach your ongoing spiritual education. Keep an open mind to new ideas, be willing to evaluate your beliefs, and revel in the joy of the spiritual journey.

Remember that the purpose of spiritual education isn't to arrive at a destination or to have all the answers. Instead, it's about getting involved in the journey itself - a voyage of growth, discovery, and deeper connection. So, go forward with an open heart and a questioning mind, and accept spirituality as a lifetime experience.

13.2 Adapting and Growing Your Spiritual Practices

It's natural for your spiritual practices to change and evolve as you go through life. Your road will not always be a straight line, like a river that bends and twists on its way to the sea. It is your adaptability and readiness to evolve that molds and deepens your spiritual path.

Beginning a spiritual journey often entails experimenting with various practices, studying different routes, and gradually discovering what resonates with you. Some behaviors may become obsolete as time passes, while others may take on greater significance. The meditation practice you initially found difficult may turn out to be a source of great serenity and reflection. Alternatively, you can discover a new spiritual tradition that aligns with your growing views and experiences.

However, it is critical to remember that change should occur naturally rather than forcefully. It is acceptable if your procedures do not alter substantially or rapidly. Spiritual development can sometimes require deepening existing practices rather than embracing new ones. It's about going deeper, peeling back layers, and seeing an old practice in a new way.

Other times, life events may force you to make big changes in your spiritual habits. These could be happy events like the birth of a child or marriage, or sad events like illness or the death of a loved one. Such occurrences have the potential to radically alter our perspectives of and need for spiritual support. During stressful circumstances, for example, you may find solace in activities that promote strength and resilience, such as grounding meditations or nurturing self-care rituals.

The key is to stay open and sensitive, to listen to your heart's whispers, and to trust your intuition. It's not about following the current spiritual trend or doing what everyone else is doing. It's about respecting your individual spiritual journey.

Maintaining a spirit of curiosity and readiness to learn is also beneficial. Maintain an open mind to new ideas, teachings, and practices. Participate in seminars, study books, listen to speakers, and connect with spiritual communities. You never know where or when you could come upon something that sparks your spirit and propels you forward.

Finally, keep in mind that spirituality is a journey rather than a destination. And, like every journey, it has ups and downs, twists and turns, starts and finishes. Accept everything. Because it is only by navigating these shifts, adapting to the currents, and expanding your spiritual practices that you can genuinely engage with the journey and return to your actual self.

13.3 Recognizing and Celebrating Spiritual Growth

The business of day-to-day living often makes it difficult to recognize the subtle and slow changes that occur in one's spiritual development. It is not necessarily denoted by prominent landmarks or by dramatic changes. On the spiritual path, growth is frequently indicated by seemingly insignificant shifts in attitude or behavior. Recognizing and honoring these milestones along the way is an essential part of your spiritual path; doing so will help you stay motivated and give you a better appreciation for the progress you've already achieved.

Self-awareness is the first step in recognizing one's own spiritual progress. As you continue to engage in spiritual activities, you will begin to become aware of gradual changes occurring within your thoughts, feelings, and actions. It's possible that you'll notice that you react differently to the kinds of events that used to bother you. Despite the difficulties that life throws at you, you can find that you have a deeper sense of serenity and satisfaction. Alternately, you could experience a heightened sense of connection and empathy towards the people and the planet that are surrounding you.

There is no requirement for spectacular displays while commemorating these shifts in circumstance. Taking a minute to recognize and be grateful for the progress you've made is an important part of this. It might be as easy as taking a moment to be grateful first thing in the morning or writing in a journal about the lessons you've learned from your experiences.

Keep in mind that the process of spiritual development does not follow a straight path. There will be times when you make a significant headway, and other times when it will feel as though you are making no headway at all. It's also possible that you'll go through phases that feel like a step backward. This is only one more step along the path. When faced with challenges of this nature, it is important to think back to where you came from and acknowledge the progress that has been made.

The fact that spirituality is so deeply ingrained in a person's life is one of the many wonderful things about it. The path that one takes toward spiritual enlightenment is unique to them, just as their development is. Therefore, while it might be beneficial to have spiritual mentors or groups for the purpose of guidance and support, it is important to avoid comparing your own growth with that of other people. Your journey is your own, and every step forward, no matter how tiny, is something to be proud of and a reason to celebrate.

When you acknowledge and celebrate the progress you've made in your spiritual life, you are not only recognizing the fact that you've come a long way, but you are also strengthening your resolve to continue on the path. You are reiterating your commitment to a life filled with never-ending learning, adventure, and discovery. So, stop what you're doing for a second, acknowledge how far you've come, and find joy in the wondrous path of spiritual development that lies ahead of you.

CHAPTER 14: CONTRIBUTING TO A SPIRITUAL COMMUNITY

14.1 The Role of Community in Spirituality

Human beings have an instinctive need to connect with other people and have a sense of belonging in a group because we are social creatures by nature. This holds true in the area of spirituality exactly the same way as it does in every other facet of life. Indeed, the role of community in spirituality is varied, serving as a supportive network in times of difficulty, a collective force for positive change, and an environment that is conducive to personal development and growth.

A shared sense of purpose and belonging is one of the most significant advantages that comes from being a part of a spiritual community. Being a part of a community of people who share similar values and perspectives, whether it be a local meditation group, an online spiritual discussion forum, or a global humanitarian movement, provides a profound sense of connection. This is true whether the community in question is online or offline. Knowing that you are not alone on your spiritual journey may be a source of tremendous solace as well as inspiration.

In addition, spiritual communities can provide vital direction and support. These groups can be a source of instruction and mentorship for individuals who are new to spirituality, assisting them in navigating the wide landscape that is composed of spiritual practices and ideologies. These events provide chances for more in-depth inquiry, conversation, and reflection for practitioners with a greater level of experience. When faced with uncertainty or challenges, the wisdom and compassion shared by members of the community can serve as a guiding light and source of support.

However, the function of a spiritual community goes beyond merely fostering personal development and providing emotional support. Transformation on an individual level is only one aspect of what it is to be spiritual; equally important is making a positive impact on the world around us. As a consequence of this, spiritual communities have the potential to function as influential agents of societal change. Collective actions have the potential to make a tremendous influence, whether they are directed toward the promotion of peace, the advocacy of environmentally sustainable practices, or the provision of assistance to people who are in need.

In the same way, participating in the activities of a spiritual community and contributing to it are both necessary aspects of a person's journey toward spiritual enlightenment. When we lend a helping hand to others, exchange perspectives, and collaborate on the accomplishment of shared objectives, we frequently broaden our understanding of both us and the spiritual pathways we follow. When we give, we open ourselves up to receiving.

To be a part of a spiritual community, however, does not necessitate adhering to a predetermined religion's doctrines or rituals, and this is an essential point to keep in mind. Authentic spiritual communities recognize and appreciate the value of diversity. They promote open communication, personal exploration, and a respectful attitude toward all possible routes.

A spiritual community might be thought of as a garden, with each member serving as a distinct flower that adds their own special charm to the overall splendor of the living, dynamic, and ever-changing whole. It is a place where individuals can grow on an individual level while also contributing to the growth of the group as a whole, thus nurturing a communal garden of spiritual enlightenment, love, and oneness.

14.2 Encouraging and Supporting Others on Their Spiritual Journeys

The journey along the spiritual road is one that is very personal and one that is distinct for each and every one of us. Nevertheless, this does not imply that we must travel without any companions. Because we are members of a spiritual community, we have the honor and the duty to cheer on and assist the spiritual development of our fellow believers on their own paths. When we do this, we contribute to the growth of the group, enhancing the spirituality that we all share together while also enhancing our personal capacity for understanding and empathy.

There are many different ways to support other people on their individual spiritual paths. When someone is struggling with spiritual concerns or issues, you could help them by just lending an ear to listen to what they have to say. Sharing your own experiences, thoughts, or resources that you've discovered to be beneficial could fall under this category. Keep in mind that encouraging someone does not mean pressuring them to adopt a particular perspective or behavior. It is important to create an atmosphere of acceptance and motivation for them so that they can delve further into their spirituality.

The act of encouraging someone is a natural progression that naturally leads to supporting them on their spiritual journey. This could involve providing emotional support during difficult times, providing practical help such as suggesting relevant books or courses, or even engaging in spiritual activities together, such as meditating or praying together.

When it comes to providing spiritual assistance for other people, you must walk a tight line. It is necessary to respect the individual liberty and distinct spiritual journey of each person. If you try to "fix" someone else's spiritual issues or offer unsolicited counsel, you will likely end up making the situation worse rather than improving it. Instead, make it your mission to offer compassionate and non-judgmental support in the hopes of assisting the person in question in feeling understood, validated, and empowered in their pursuit of spirituality.

It is not just the people who are on the receiving end of encouragement and support who benefit from these behaviors. In addition to this, it serves as a potent impetus for the development of our own spirituality. When we are able to explain our grasp of spiritual concepts to others, it not only enhances our ability to empathize with others, but it also broadens our viewpoint. In addition to this, it acts as a mirror for our own path, reflecting back to us our own uncertainties, breakthroughs, and transitions.

In addition to this, it generates a virtuous cycle of positive feedback inside the spiritual community. The more we help others, the greater the likelihood that they will help us in return. This helps to create an environment that is conducive to the growth, understanding, and unity of all parties involved.

Keep in mind that any spiritual journey, including the one you are on right now, is a continuing process that is full of twists and turns, as well as highs and lows. We may make these trips less intimidating and more enriching for both us and others if we cultivate an attitude of encouragement and support for one another. As you make your way along the spiritual road, remember to keep an eye out for other people on the journey and to give a helping hand to them. Because, when it comes down to it, we're all in this together.

14.3 Engaging in Service and Contribution

The notion of service and contribution is a basic component of many spiritual traditions. Serving others and contributing to the well-being of our communities and the world at large is a manifestation of the love, compassion, and connectivity that our spiritual practices create. We often obtain the deepest spiritual revelations and fulfillment when we give.

Spiritual service is more than just spectacular gestures or large-scale humanitarian operations. It can be as simple and meaningful as offering a stranger a smile, listening to a buddy in need, or volunteering your time to improve your local community. These simple acts of kindness can create a tsunami of positive change and strengthen our sense of togetherness.

There are countless ways to provide service and help others.

A powerful method to give back is to volunteer your time and energy to organizations that connect with your spiritual ideals. This could include volunteering at a food bank, teaching meditation to neighborhood organizations, or participating in environmental conservation efforts.

Financial or material donations can also be used to provide service. Every contribution counts, whether it's to a charity that helps poor children, providing books to a community library, or financing the planting of trees to offset carbon emissions.

However, one of the most powerful forms of service is passing on spiritual knowledge and practices to others. Sharing your spiritual understanding, whether by writing, speaking, or simply modeling spiritual values in your daily life, has the potential to make a big difference in the lives of others. Remember, it's not about preaching or converting others to your point of view, but about sharing insights that can help others on their own spiritual journeys.

Service and contribution are also effective tools for personal spiritual growth. It leads us beyond our narrow self-interest and assists us in embodying the spiritual ideas we value. It fosters attributes such as empathy, selflessness, and kindness. Furthermore, it provides our spiritual practice a greater purpose by grounding it in the reality of human experience and our world's urgent demands.

"Service is the rent we pay for being. It is the very purpose of life, not something you do in your leisure time." - Marian Wright Edelman

Allow your spiritual journey to motivate you to serve and contribute in ways that are meaningful to you and watch how it enriches your path and the world around you.

CHAPTER 15: LOOKING FORWARD: YOUR SPIRITUAL FUTURE

15.1 Planning for Future Spiritual Exploration

As we progress further along in our spiritual journeys, we can discover that we start to speculate about what lies in store for us. The beauty of spirituality lies in the fact that it is not a destination but rather a path of constant growth and self-discovery that continues throughout one's entire life. But how exactly can we organize ourselves for such a free-form and introspective trip? Let's go right down to that.

To begin, it is of the utmost importance to keep in mind that our spiritual path will progress just as we do. What strikes a chord with us now might not strike the same chord tomorrow. This is totally normal and represents the nature of our consciousness, which is always developing further. Consequently, the creation of a formal road map is not necessary while making plans for future spiritual study. Instead, we should focus on cultivating a mindset that is open, curious, and willing to explore new frontiers of our inner world.

Setting spiritual intentions is one method of making plans. In contrast to objectives, which are centered on accomplishments, intentions are concerned with how we desire to manifest ourselves during the course of our spiritual journey. They are the characteristics that we aspire to embody, the principles that we wish to guide our lives by, or the mystical encounters that we wish to bring into our lives. For instance, one of our intentions could be to increase the amount of self-love we practice, to hone our meditation skills, or to investigate different religious practices.

Another essential component of planning is to schedule time in your schedule for regular periods of introspection. This could involve writing in a journal about our spiritual experiences, insights, and struggles, or it could just consist of spending solitary time reflecting on our spiritual journey. These activities have the potential to assist us in remaining in tune with our ever-evolving spiritual requirements and goals, thereby directing our ongoing investigations.

One further essential component of planning is ensuring that our pursuit of spiritual enlightenment remains unabated. This could include engaging in activities such as reading books on spirituality, going to seminars or retreats, being a part of a community of spiritual seekers, or seeking advice from a spiritual guide. Learning new things on a consistent basis makes our spiritual path interesting, deepens our comprehension, and enables us to see things from fresh angles.

As a last point of consideration, it is critical that we work on developing our capacity for patience as well as self-compassion as we plan our future spiritual inquiry. To make spiritual progress, we must frequently traverse difficult terrain, face our shadow selves, and push the boundaries of our comfort zones. Because this is a voyage that takes place in its own time, it cannot be hurried along. Therefore, be kind to yourself, recognize that your pace is appropriate, and applaud your success, no matter how seemingly insignificant it may be.

Developing a malleable structure that can accommodate our ever-increasing maturity should be the focus of our planning for our future spiritual journey. It's about cultivating a fruitful ground so that our spirituality can grow deeper and more expansive in step with our constantly shifting consciousness. According to the well-known spiritual author Thomas Merton, "the spiritual journey is neither a career nor a success story." It is a series of minor humiliations of the false self that, as they accumulate, become increasingly profound. Therefore, commit to the voyage with an open mind, a sense of wonder, and compassion, and have faith in the course that is opening up before you.

15.2 Spirituality and Aging: Growing into Wisdom

As we become older, we inevitably acquire new experiences, viewpoints, and priorities. Things that we once thought were crucial may now appear to be unimportant, while things that we ignored may turn out to have increased significance. Many people, at this point in their lives, become interested in spiritual matters and open themselves up to the chances for development and enlightenment that this period of life presents.

Growing older gives a richness of experience, and with this wealth of knowledge comes wisdom. Aging brings these two things together. It presents a priceless chance for us to advance our spiritual awareness, broaden our consciousness, and achieve a profound sense of serenity and contentment in our lives as a result of doing so. In a lovely expression, the poet Rumi put it this way: "The wiser you become, the less you speak." When you love someone more, you demand less of them. When it comes to giving, the more you put out, the more you get back. These sentiments, taken as a whole, beautifully represent the profound religious comprehension that can come with advancing years.

Aging and the experiences that come with it, such as coming to terms with our own mortality, watching our physical capacities shift, and grieving the death of loved ones, can be powerful catalysts for personal growth and development on a spiritual level. They prompt us to dig farther than the surface, beyond the tangible, in order to search for meaning and comprehension on a more profound level. They serve as a reminder of the transience that characterizes existence.

We are able to negotiate these problems with grace and acceptance as we age and employ the rising spiritual understanding that we have gained. We can create a profound sense of acceptance and calm inside ourselves by engaging in spiritual activities such as meditation, mindfulness, and prayer. This will allow us to welcome the inevitable changes that come with advancing years rather than fighting against them. We may cultivate the mindset that our physical bodies are only vehicles for our spiritual journeys, and we can learn to love and care for our bodies even as they age and undergo change.

Elders are respected as the keepers of wisdom and spiritual insight in many different religious and spiritual traditions. At this point in our lives, we are able to put our spiritual knowledge to use not only for our own development but also to direct and encourage the development of the spiritual paths of those around us. We are in a position to make significant contributions to the spiritual development of our communities, whether via the communication of our observations and experiences, the provision of emotional support, or the simple modeling of a life that is spiritually enriched.

Consequently, growing older is not a sign of decline but rather of elevation; it is an opportunity to advance to new levels of spiritual awareness and fulfillment. It is a time when we are able to reflect back on our path with gratitude, savor the depth of the present moment, and look forward to the further spiritual development that lies ahead of us. Therefore, as you go into this new phase of life, try to view it as a significant spiritual opportunity. This is a time for you to mature spiritually, increase the depth of your spiritual awareness, and appreciate the splendor and richness of life.

15.3 Leaving a Spiritual Legacy

Our spiritual journey is not just about our own personal development and enlightenment, but also about the mark we make on the world around us as we go along this path. Our spiritual legacy consists of how those around us are impacted by our deeds, our words, our acts of compassion, and our love for one another.

Nevertheless, what exactly does it mean to leave behind a spiritual legacy? It is not about being remembered for great achievements or building something that will remain in existence for all of time. Instead, it is about having a positive impact on the lives of other people and the world around us, which is born out of the spiritual ideas and practices that we uphold.

Every day, the decisions we make and the deeds we do contribute to the legacy we leave behind on a spiritual level. When we are compassionate and kind to other people, we set off a chain reaction whose effects are felt well beyond our own sphere of influence. When we lead genuine lives that are centered on the principles that we hold most dear, we motivate others to do the same in their own lives. When we make a contribution to the communities in which we live, whether that contribution takes the form of mentoring, volunteering, or simply being there for someone who is in need, we have a modest but substantial impact on the world.

The act of passing on our spiritual knowledge and experiences to others is one way to leave behind a legacy on the spiritual plane. Writing, instructing, mentoring, or even just having deep talks with the people we care about can all fall under this category. Through the act of imparting our wisdom to others, we can facilitate their progress on their individual spiritual paths and add to their level of comprehension.

It is also about the impact that we have on the world when we talk about leaving a spiritual legacy. This could include working to promote social justice, promoting environmental sustainability, or giving to causes that are important to us. It is about putting our resources, such as our time, energy, and abilities, as well as our material wealth, to use so that we can make the world a better place.

In the end, leaving a spiritual legacy is about living a life that represents our most fundamental ideals and goals in the here and now. Being the change, we hope to see in the world, and having a significant impact on the lives of others, is at the heart of this movement. It is about making waves of love, kindness, and wisdom that will continue to spread even after we are no longer here.

Therefore, when you look forward to the spiritual future that lies ahead of you, think about the legacy that you hope to leave behind. Ask yourself, "How can I live my spirituality in ways that enrich the lives of others and the world?" and then think about the answers. Always keep in mind that the legacy you leave behind is shaped by every act of love you perform, every piece of advice you share, and every genuine moment you share with others. As you move forward on your spiritual journey, remember to do so not only for yourself but also for all the others whose lives you will impact along the road.

IN CONCLUSION...

As we come to the end of our trip together, it is important to keep in mind that the core of spirituality is not about arriving at a particular destination but rather about enjoying the wonderful, sometimes difficult, and always enlightening journey of self-discovery and progress. A spiritual life consists of a never-ending dedication to the cultivation of self-love, comprehension, and a more profound connection with the cosmos.

You are about to embark on a journey that will push you to your limits, present you with difficult challenges, and possibly even split you open. You will discover your greatest power, your deepest insight, and your most profound connection to the divine during those moments when you are bursting open. Yet, this does not mean that you will not experience any discomfort during this process. It is through resiliency that we are able to emerge stronger, it is through hardship that we can find our actual talents, and it is through love and kindness that we are able to leave an impact on the world that is both meaningful and long-lasting.

Keep in mind that there is more than one way to achieve enlightenment on a spiritual level as you continue your path toward spiritual growth. The things that we go through, the beliefs that we hold, and the goals that we strive to achieve each contribute to the formation of our own paths. Embrace the journey ahead of you with both your heart and intellect wide open. Be curious, be courageous, and most all, be compassionate, both toward yourself and toward other people.

Have faith in the process, even if the road ahead looks rough. Even when we are unsure of where we are going, the cosmos has a way of directing us. Always keep in mind that you are never on this path alone. Every action you take along your spiritual path influences the bigger picture because you are a part of a magnificent web of life in which everything is related to everything else.

As you move along your road, don't forget to give your spiritual being the nourishment it needs daily. Your spiritual self, like a plant, needs frequent practices of meditation, awareness, and self-reflection in order to develop. Just as a plant needs water and sunlight to grow, so does your spiritual self. Rather than viewing these routines as chores or responsibilities, look at them as priceless chances to strengthen your bond with your true self and the cosmos.

The spiritual path is not always an easy one to travel, but the benefits of doing so are beyond measure. As you progress in your spiritual practice, you will discover a sense of calm and contentment that is unaffected by the conditions of your exterior environment. You'll find a wellspring of inner strength that enables you to face the hardships of life with poise and resiliency, which will be revealed to you. And maybe most importantly, you will have the opportunity to experience love and connection, both of which will infuse your life with joy and meaning.

Keep in mind that you are not traveling the path of enlightenment alone. Give them the benefit of your experiences, your knowledge, and your affection. Your progress on the spiritual path has the potential to encourage and uplift those around you. You, in turn, will draw motivation from their travels, gain wisdom from them, and find support in them.

Although we are nearing the conclusion of one book, we are just starting a new one. The beginning of your spiritual journey is just beginning to unravel. Have faith in the process, give yourself over to love, and remember that the universe is on your side. Engage the future with a positive outlook, a strong will, love, and kindness. Shine as brightly as you can because the world needs the light that only you can bring.

Continue to broaden your horizons, develop yourself, and travel the path of your spirituality with dignity and fortitude. Always keep in mind that your spirituality is the source of your power, your way, and the gift you provide to the world. Invest in it, care for it, and then let it shine.

I wish you the best of luck on your journey. It is a privilege to travel this road beside you. Let us move forward as a group with love, hope, and faith in the spiritual future that we share as a community. Always keep in mind that the universe has an amazing destiny in store for you. Trust, surrender, and let your spiritual journey emerge.

ABOUT THE AUTHOR

Brooke Sims

Brooke Sims is an American author who grew up in Texas but now resides in the Blue Ridge Mountains in the gorgeous state of North Carolina with her husband, and two fur babies. Brooke enjoys spending time with her four grown children. She loves all things nature, including hiking, biking, gardening, and visiting waterfalls for inspiration. She attended the University of Texas at Arlington and studied psychology and business. Brooke's significant involvement in the medical field allowed her to recognize the profound desire and necessity for both comfort and mental health among her patients. Through her extensive experience, she came to understand how important it is for individuals to have access to support that addresses their emotional well-being in conjunction with their physical health. Her journey to calmness started with the death of her father while attending college. She realized she needed to find balance in order to enjoy all facets of life.

BOOKS BY THIS AUTHOR

Balancing Act: Navigating The Anxiously Calm Mind 52-Week Journal